The River and the Mountain:

The Solo Developer's Handbook

W. S. Matis

The River and the Mountain: The Solo Developer's Handbook

International Cataloging-in-Publication Data (CIP)

(Câmara Brasileira do Livro, SP - Brasil)

Matis, W. S.
The river and the mountain : the solo developer's handbook / W. S. Matis. -- 1st ed -- Betim, MG : Author's Edition, 2025.

ISBN 978-65-01-64560-5

1. Entrepreneurs 2. Entrepreneurship 3. Games - Development 4. Programming (Computers) 5. Projects - Development 6. Software - Development I. Title.

25-294594.0 CDD-005.1068

Indexes for systematic cataloging:

1. Software: Development: Projects: Management: Computer Science 005.1068

Maria Alice Ferreira - Librarian - CRB-8/7964

If you wait for company

You may never start your journey

W. S. Matis

Table of Contents

Chapter 1: Introduction to Solo Development

Whenever I start reading a book by a new author, the first questions that come to mind are: Who is this person? Is he a fake guru or something? If you're wondering the same thing right now, I don't blame you. Snake oil salesmen[1] are quite common these days and spread like wildfire across the internet. But rest assured, I'm not here to teach you how to "get rich quick" or how to be successful. After all, I'm not rich (at least not yet), and I'm not as successful as I would like to be for my age.

So why am I writing a book about solo development? Well, as of this writing, I have already created, developed, and published 46 projects[2] as a solo developer, and I have been living exclusively off the revenue generated by these projects for the past six years.

I don't mean to brag, really, I'm just a regular guy, trying to make a living and support my family. There are far more talented and successful solo developers out there who have achieved greater results in the same amount of time, or even less. I look up to them with admiration and respect, and I know that if I stay true to my path, one day I will reach the same level or go even further.

But on the other hand, there are also people struggling to finish what they started and giving up after getting lost in the middle of a project. If, by sharing the little I know, I end up helping even a single person in this situation, I'll consider this book a success.

In this book, I'll share everything I have learned working full-time as a solo developer for the past six years. I'll cover fundamental topics like project

---

[1] Also known as scammers or con artists

[2] Including games and game assets for Unity™ and Unreal Engine™

management and product design in simplified, beginner-friendly language, making it as accessible as possible to everyone, regardless of proficiency level. I'll also share some tips and tricks on how to avoid the pitfalls of solo development and keep pushing forward towards your goals.

By the end of the book, you'll be familiarized with a simplified workflow I have developed to build a small business as a solo developer. And if you're still feeling unsure and lost by then, just remember: every successful person was a beginner at some point.

1.1. My Journey as a Solo Developer

My name is Warley and I am the solo developer behind WSM Game Studio[3]. For the past six years I have been making a living as a solo indie developer in the games industry. But how did I get here?

I have been passionate about games since I was a child, and since my teenage years, I have already known that someday I would like to start my own business. I attended the public school system, which is definitely not designed to prepare aspiring entrepreneurs, especially within the broken education system of a third world country. However, I have always tried my best to be a good student, to the point that most people who know me think that I have always been the smart kid, able to learn quickly and understand things easily. But in reality, I also struggle with complex concepts and solving difficult problems like everyone else.

The truth is, I have always been the "try harder" type. For some reason, I have insane levels of resilience, so when things get rough, I just keep trying again and again, until I find a solution. Maybe all this resilience came from playing old

[3] https://wsmgamestudio.com/

school games, I'm from the 90s, games back then weren't designed to be a walk in the park, they were designed to be fun and challenging[4].

In my early twenties, I received a scholarship for a bachelor's degree in IT at a renowned private university. I could have applied for a game development course instead, but since I live in a third world country with very few opportunities in that field, entering the software development industry seemed like a safer option at the time.

I worked in the software development industry for a few years, and around 2016, I started studying game development in my spare time. I worked for a large tech company and at least 12 hours of my time were consumed by work and public transportation on a typical day. I was constantly tired, but I knew that if I didn't do anything, I would be stuck in that cycle forever.

Since opportunities in the gaming industry are scarce, especially for beginners, I decided to create my own opportunities. So, by the end of 2017, I left my job to become an entrepreneur in the gaming industry. Initially, I didn't plan on becoming a solo developer, but the few people I knew who were also interested in game development weren't willing to take the risk, so I was completely on my own.

At first, I was completely lost and unprepared. The public education system is not designed to teach people how to think or make money on their own. On the contrary, it is designed to turn people into replaceable cogs, slowly degrading into someone else's money printing machine.

Around that time, the indie game market was booming. Game engines[5] like Unity™ and Unreal Engine™, facilitated and democratized game development by

---

[4] Contrary to popular belief, gaming isn't just a useless hobby; most people I know who grew up playing video games end up developing important life skills, like learning foreign languages and developing advanced problem-solving skills.

[5] A game engine is a software used for developing games

offering free licensing tiers for beginners and small studios. Indie-friendly platforms, like Steam™[6], also lowered the distribution barrier, allowing indie games to reach people all over the world. I saw a window of opportunity and, even though I was unprepared, decided to take a leap of faith. It was extremely reckless, and I won't sugarcoat it; it was like jumping out of a plane and trying to build a parachute mid-air.

My initial plan was to create a series of small indie games and publish them on Steam. I sketched out some ideas and started working on a few prototypes, but none of them looked promising. I was also bombarded with job offers on a daily basis, which was really discouraging. After a few weeks of failed prototypes, I accepted a temporary job and went back to working on my projects in my spare time. This was a huge setback for me, as I hadn't released any games yet, it felt like I was giving up before properly trying. By the time my temporary contract ended, I had a racing game prototype that was fun to play and looked promising, so I decided to fully commit this time and only consider taking another job after finishing and publishing this game.

This time, I took a more professional approach and developed a business plan. Since I was working alone, I knew the game couldn't be huge, otherwise it would take years to finish the project. So, my long-term plan was to create a racing game franchise, starting with a small simple game. Then, reuse all the content to create the next game, and repeat this process, gradually increasing the size and complexity for each new title added to the franchise.

The idea was to use the revenue generated by the previous games to fund the development of the next one. It seemed like a good plan, but halfway through the development of the first game, I realized that this plan had a huge flaw: if the first game failed to generate revenue, I wouldn't be able to fund the next one.

---

[6] https://store.steampowered.com/

Considering that an unknown indie developer's first game is statistically likely to generate little to no revenue, I was setting myself up for failure. That day, I realized I was spending months crafting a lottery ticket, that I would scratch on the release date and let luck do the rest. As an entrepreneur, you can't rely on luck; you either make your own luck or you fail. So I knew the only way for me to continue working for myself, would be to monetize the business before finishing the game. I went back to the planning board and started looking for a solution that would allow me to make money without hindering the game's development progress.

The solution ended up being very similar to my long-term strategy, but with short to medium-term profit potential. If building a franchise is only possible by dividing it into multiple smaller projects, why not divide those projects into smaller pieces as well?

From that point on, whenever I developed a new feature for the game, instead of making it exclusively for this project, I designed it as its own separate system, which could be used not only by me, but also by other game developers. I changed my perspective: instead of just creating a game, I started creating solutions for game developers, and people are willing to pay for good solutions. That's how I became a game asset developer[7].

Under this new strategy, I was able to complete my first commercial game project. It was officially released on September 6th, 2019. Although the majority of player feedback was positive, the game failed to reach a larger audience. At that point, this was expected, as it is the reality of most indie games. It was a financial failure, but I learned a lot on this journey. Working on all stages of a project, from idea conception to launch, is an incredibly enriching experience, not only from a technical point of view but also from a business perspective. I've also

---

[7] Game assets is the technical term used to describe the contents and systems that compose a game.

learned that it's easier to build something useful than something entertaining. Entertainment is subjective, usefulness is not.

By the time the game launched, the assets that emerged from the project were already generating enough revenue for me to continue my journey as a solo developer. From that point on, I decided to halt the plan of creating a game franchise and focus on the game assets market. Creating game assets is not easy or fun, but the harsh reality is that work is not supposed to be fun, it is supposed to be profitable. If something is easy and fun to do, no one is going to pay you to do it, they are going to do it themselves. So having the technical skills to do something that is hard, but necessary, makes you a valuable professional.

While I love playing video games, making them for a living as a solo developer is really challenging. However, with the particular set of skills I have developed on this journey, I'm now able to create valuable tools to help other developers succeed where I failed: building a successful game.

1.2. The River and The Mountain

Some experiences in life are so unique, that it is hard to describe what they feel like without using an allegory. That's the case for the experience of becoming a solo entrepreneur: there's a massive difference between working a regular job and starting your own business.

The job market is like a river: people drifting slowly downstream, dreaming about the day they will finally reach the sea, so they can sit comfortably on the beach and wait for the sunset of their lives. Sure, it's not always a pleasant journey: the water gets colder and the current gets stronger from time to time. But most of them aren't here by choice, they were pushed into the water and the river is all they've ever known. Not everyone is going to reach the beach in the end, but that's the dream.

Creating a business is like climbing up a mountain: it requires a lot of effort and awareness on every step of the way. Every crack you hold and every rock you step on can either lead you up toward your goals or down toward inevitable doom. Having previous climbing experience or good climbing gear may increase your chances of success, but let's not get ahead of ourselves yet.

Imagine you are drifting down the river, as you look up you can see mountains in the distance, far beyond a dense forest. Unlike most people, you don't want to retire on a beach. Instead, you would like to build a comfortable wooden cabin on top of a mountain and watch the horizon from up there as you grow old. But from the river, all of this feels just like a distant dream. You may even find others who share the same dream, but most of them are not willing to take the risk of embarking on a journey to the mountains. Deep down, you know that if you do nothing, the current will continue to drag you away, as the river takes care of everything. This is the path of least resistance: you won't have to take action, but you won't be able to choose your path either. Your only hope of fulfilling your dream is to start making your own decisions.

To reach the base of the mountain, first you need to get out of the river. However, as you start swimming, others may bump into you, making it harder for you to resist the current. You will realize how difficult it is to follow a different path. After all, it is the first time you're actually swimming, rather than floating like everyone else.

When you finally get off the water, the cold wind sends shivers down your spine as you gaze at the dense dark forest ahead. This is the moment of truth: returning to the river is the safest option, as you are still soaking wet, but if you decide to take the risk, it would be wise to bring some fish and water to increase your chances of survival.

The journey through the dark forest is exactly as it looks from the outside: if you have no survival skills, you will rely solely on your instincts to get through.

This is the hardest part of your journey, as you may get lost or even perish along the way. The nights are especially harsh, as you will be constantly haunted by your doubts. This is the period when your business is not yet profitable. It is normal to feel lost and unsure at this point, some may even give up and return to the river, but others persevere and are able to reach the other side.

Once you reach the mountains, you're no longer lost, you know exactly which direction to go, and that direction is up. You're relieved to be out of the forest, but that doesn't mean things will get any easier, you'll just have more clarity, as you're no longer obscured by the shadow of the trees.

At the base of your chosen mountain, you may meet other aspiring climbers. As you look around, you will notice some of them have prior climbing experience, some have good quality equipment, climbing partners, instructors or even sponsors. On the other hand, there are also people without any equipment at all, planning to climb with their bare hands and feet only. It is not a level playing field, life isn't fair game after all, we don't get to choose the cards we are given, we can only play the ones we got. This is the time to reassess your situation and prepare yourself to start climbing. If you have the resources, it is a good idea to acquire professional gear or training sessions. It is also a good opportunity to meet new people, as they are also interested in the same mountain. Sharing information may be mutually beneficial, just be careful, not everyone is friendly, some may gladly help, while others may try to make you fall, but the vast majority are just indifferent, they are just focused on their own journeys and there is nothing wrong with it.

The mountain is the market you are getting into: every mountain is unique and has its own level of difficulty. The skills and resources necessary for climbing, as well as the risks involved, vary not only based on the mountain, but also on how high you currently are, as each climbing section has its own sets of challenges and difficulties.

There are also camping sections along the way, where you can stop to appreciate the view and prepare yourself for the next climbing section. Every project is a climbing section, and camping is the time between projects. When camping, you need to reassess your situation and decide whether to climb higher, go down or build your cabin where you stand. If you don't have the resources necessary for building your cabin yet, you need to keep climbing and gathering more resources as you go. But don't forget to appreciate the view from time to time, it is the only thing that makes climbing worth the risk.

If you came from a family of professional climbers, you might inherit a cabin or grow up training to conquer your own mountain someday. But if you came from the river, your first project isn't at the base of the mountain, it is within those dark woods. That's why so many people fail to finish their first project: without guidance, it's easier to get lost. You can think of this book as a compass: it doesn't always point towards the direction you should go[8], but if you use it correctly, it will help you find your own path.

1.3. The Best Time in History to Work on a Solo Project

Thanks to the internet, it has never been easier to learn a new skill or to reach potential clients all around the globe. It is the best time in history to build a one-person business, but most people are so distracted that they don't even realize that. The internet can be an endless source of distractions or a valuable font of information, it is just a tool, the final result depends on how you use it.

With the rise of digital products[9], all you need to start a digital business is a computer connected to the internet, learn the technical skills required and understand your niche. For example, some platforms allow individuals to host

[8] Unless you are going north

[9] For example games, e-books, digital art, project templates, software, etc

digital products free of charge, in return, the platform profits by taking a small cut of every sale. You just need to create an account and have something ready to sell, the platform only makes money when you do, so it is a win-win situation for everyone. This lowered the barrier of entry of many markets and created amazing opportunities for individuals that would never get a chance otherwise.

Some niches also benefit from having free software to work with. This is the case for software developers for example: most software development tools are either free or offer free licensing tiers for beginners and small businesses. Users are only required to upgrade to paid a subscription, after reaching a high annual revenue threshold. Therefore, only successful businesses are required to pay. But if the tool was used to achieve success, this is more than fair.

There has also been a shift in the education industry, with online education platforms allowing teachers all over the world to offer short courses focused on developing a single skill. This has made education more affordable and customizable: it is now possible to invest time and money learning only exactly what you need for your project. It is like building your own customized curriculum under demand.

Building your own curriculum may seem difficult at first, but that's only because the formal education system is not designed to make people independent, on the contrary, throughout the system you are told what you should learn. We are not trained to be able to learn for ourselves, we are trained to obey a figure of authority. In the early years, this is necessary, as children are not mature enough to decide which is the best for them, if left on their own, they will not learn how to read or do basic math.

However, in an optimal scenario, after going through the education system, young adults should be able to think for themselves, which isn't the case for most people. But don't get me wrong, although the formal education system is flawed, it is still important to complete it. Just be aware that if you want to excel as a professional, your learning journey doesn't end with graduation. In fact, the first day after graduation is just the first day of the rest of your life: you are now free to choose which skills to learn, and knowing how to make that decision is crucial for your future.

To make the most of this new era of education, you need to develop two skills. The first one is the ability to choose your own path. But, if you're planning to work on your own project, you may already have this skill. The other one, is the ability of filtering useful information.

There is a massive amount of information on the internet, but statistically, most of it is either inaccurate or is irrelevant to you. This also applies to online courses, as there are malicious individuals selling fake or low quality information for profit. When choosing an online course, you should always choose platforms that have a reliable review system so you can identify which tutors are trustworthy[10]. You should also avoid purchasing large course bundles just because they're on sale. More often than not, people won't watch all the courses in a bundle, and even if they do, they won't put most of it into practical use. It is better to acquire only the information that you need and will put it to practical use in the near future.

I like to define this as "learning under demand": the ability to focus on learning only what you need to solve the problems you currently have and ignore all the rest. Learning under demand is one of the most valuable skills for any professional. This not only turns you into a problem solving machine, but also prevents you from wasting time and money learning stuff you are never going to use in your life.

---

[10] Avoid purchasing courses directly from the tutor's website and avoid platforms that don't support written customer reviews

This new era of self-education and digital products, created a new market in which even solo entrepreneurs are able to thrive. It's now possible to learn skills, create products and put them for sale, all from the comfort of your own home.

1.4. Pros & Cons of Solo Development

Finishing your first project is a major milestone on your journey. It could be the first product of your brand, the start of your professional portfolio, or even something you're building just for fun. Regardless of what it is, finishing your first project gives you the satisfaction of finally bringing your ideas to life.

However, like most valuable things in life, projects require time and effort to be built, and as a beginner, it is easier to get lost or to get stuck on unexpected problems along the way. As part of a team, other people may help you and point you in the right direction, but when you are working solo, you have to be self-sufficient and figure things out on your own. But don't worry, even though overcoming these issues by yourself may not be easy, it is not impossible.

But, if it is so hard, why would someone work as a solo developer? Well, beginners may struggle to get a job, join a team, or find a business partner. Sometimes, you have no other option, rather than building everything yourself. After all, people don't usually hire or trust someone based only on "good ideas", if you want to be respected, you need to prove your value first.

After completing your first project, you'll have something to show, and this is one of the most effective ways to prove that you're reliable and can actually get things done. It will also make it easier to land your dream job or find a business partner, if that's what you're looking for.

On the other hand, some people prefer to work solo, especially on small or personal projects. Some professions also allow people to work alone and even build small businesses. After all, a company doesn't need to be big to be lucrative, it only needs to be efficient and provide good products or services. However, working as a solo developer has pros and cons, and it's important to be aware of them before embarking on your solo journey.

Advantages of being a solo developer

- **Creative freedom:** You decide which projects to work on and which direction to follow.
- **No negative influences:** You don't need to deal with annoying or lazy co-workers.
- **No one holding you back:** There are no office politics or incompetent managers hindering your progress.
- **No corporate time sinkers:** No pointless meetings or mandatory training sessions on topics that don't interest you.
- **Flexible working hours:** You can build your routine around your most productive hours and don't need permission to rearrange your schedule to deal with emergencies.
- **Higher Earning Potential:** Income is not limited to a pre-defined paycheck, the more you produce, the more you may earn.
- **Skill Set Diversification:** You are not limited to learning the skills of a single role, you get to decide which skills to learn to expand your potential.
- **Home Office:** No need to rent an office when you work alone.
- **All the glory:** You receive all credit and profits for successful projects.

Disadvantages of being a solo developer

- **No Stable Income:** There is no guaranteed paycheck waiting for you, you need to put in the work and avoid slacking.

- **Total accountability:** You are solely responsible for all failed projects and financial losses.
- **Less Social Interactions:** If you are a social person, you may feel isolated working by yourself.
- **Home Office Issues:** Family members and pets may have a hard time respecting your working hours.
- **Wearing all the hats:** You need to manage and work on the project at the same time, which requires you to bounce between technical and administrative tasks on a daily basis.
- **Risk of Stagnation:** You are responsible for planning which skills you should learn to evolve as a professional. If you don't push yourself to keep learning, your growth potential may be limited.
- **No brainstorming sessions:** You rely exclusively on your own ideas.
- **No positive influences:** There are no skilled co-workers to learn from or to collaborate with. You have limited access to constructive feedback from other professionals.
- **Self-discipline required:** There is no one to force you to follow your schedule and respect your working hours. If you struggle with self-discipline, you need to learn how to overcome this barrier[11].

It's important to keep in mind that the pros and cons may vary depending on your individual preferences and personality traits, so it's also wise to consider any additional pros and cons that you believe would impact your solo journey.

[11] Yes, self-discipline is a skill that can be mastered

1.5. Enhancing Your Chances of Success

While a clear vision of the advantages of solo development may serve as motivation, being aware of the disadvantages is even more important to increase your chances of success. The entire concept of risk management revolves around avoiding unpleasant surprises. Identifying what could go wrong as soon as possible is crucial for planning ahead, and taking steps to mitigate or eliminate issues before they become a real threat.

From a philosophical perspective, risk management can be seen as a tool that transforms weakness into strength. Let's look at some suggestions on how to mitigate some of the disadvantages listed in the previous section.

1.5.1. Financial Stability

If you plan to make a living as a solo developer, not having a steady income at the start of your journey is the most critical issue that needs to be addressed in order for you to succeed. Fortunately, this risk can be mitigated by preparing yourself financially before embarking on your journey. Taking a temporary job to save money before starting your business may seem like a bittersweet solution, especially for those who want to work for themselves, but depending on your financial situation, it may be the only option. As an alternative, you may also take a part-time job or start your project as a side hustle. Your projects will certainly take longer to complete, but slow progress is better than no progress at all.

It's also recommended to start with small-scale projects that can be monetized. The profit from your first project may not be enough to cover your expenses, but as you launch more projects, your monthly income will gradually increase, to the point where you can quit your job and focus exclusively on your projects. This is a long-term strategy, so it requires commitment, but it's also a safe strategy for transitioning from a regular job to being your own boss.

Freelancing is also a good source of short-term income to raise money, but keep in mind that, for long term strategies like this, it is better to focus on creating a product catalog on a well-established online store. Remember, freelance gigs only pay you once per project. On the other hand, a product catalog has the potential to generate recurring income.

As a freelancer, you need to be constantly finding new projects and deal with other people's specifications: it's like having a different boss every week, but without the stability of a fixed paycheck. If you fall ill and are unable to work, this could be a huge problem. However, a well-established product catalog generates income even when you are on vacation. But don't think that building a product catalog is an infinite money glitch, you still need to launch new products and updates from time to time to extend your product catalog lifespan.

You must also keep in mind that situations in which someone's first product is a huge financial success are really rare, so it is important to keep your expectations under control. If your first product is able to generate at least a small amount of income every month, that's already a good sign you are on the right path. As you release more products, the quality of your products tend to gradually increase and that's what moves you forward.

1.5.2. Dealing with Failure

Contrary to popular belief, success is not exclusive for talented people, for normal hardworking people, success is a statistical game defined by consistency. Every new product added to your catalog works like a lottery ticket, that may change your life forever, but even though luck plays a role, you must work as if it doesn't exist and focus on increasing your catalog. If you remain consistent, over time the revenue from multiple products adds up and you start ripping the profits of your hard work.

But what about products that generate little or no profit? Well, generating a small amount of profit is not a problem, as it builds up over time. In this strategy, a product is only considered a failure if it generates no revenue at all. Initially, you may keep these products to add volume to your catalog. But, as your business grows, it's acceptable to clean up your catalog and focus exclusively on your successful products.

Failed projects are part of the journey, the market simply does not absorb everything you throw at it. Product quality and demand are two really important factors that define if a product will be accepted or not by the market. Over time, you'll learn how to evaluate demand and improve the quality of your products, but as a beginner it is better to release multiple small projects and observe the market reaction, that's a reliable way of testing new ideas, gaining experience and expanding your catalog at the same time.

That's why the MVP[12] strategy is so effective, I'll cover this strategy with more details in chapter 2. For now, just keep in mind that failing is not exclusively a bad thing. When you fail, you learn what does not work and what not to do on future projects. Negative experiences are inevitable in life, so we may as well make the best of them as learning opportunities.

1.5.3. Dealing with Solitude

Having few social interactions in your work environment is only a problem if you are a social person, for introverts, like me, and people that just want to get the job done and go home, this could actually be a blessing in disguise. But, regardless if you like it or not to make friends at work, loneliness could be an issue. The worst part is not having anyone to help you deal with work related issues, when you get stuck on a problem, you are on your own.

[12] Minimum Viable Product

Sometimes, it feels like you are lost and alone in a forest and your only hope of survival is relying on your natural instincts to find your way home. If you're not careful, loneliness can get to your head and take you to really dark places. The only way to overcome situations like this on your own, is to keep pushing forward like if your life depends on it. It may be hard in the beginning, but resilience is the key. If you keep pushing forward, your problem solving skills improve over time, making you more and more independent. Self-sufficiency is one of the most valuable and desirable professional skills anyone can have, regardless if you are working alone or as part of a team. Developing this skill will benefit both your professional and personal life.

As for the loneliness, this needs to be dealt with in your personal life. Hanging out with your friends and loved ones on the days off is important to keep a healthy work life balance. As an adult, you are also not limited to making friends exclusively in the workplace, you may also attend social events and join communities built around common hobbies. There are plenty of opportunities for meeting new people, just get out there, instead of never leaving the house.

1.5.4. Home Office Boundaries

A one-person business is all about effectiveness, in order to be viable, it must be a lean and cost effective business. A single person working from home it's the leanest it gets. The truth is, if your company is not big, you don't need to rent an office. Even big tech companies are capable of operating just fine under a remote work regime, especially when team members are scattered around the world. Any occupation that requires only a computer and internet connection is more than suitable for home office. However, family members and pets may have a hard time respecting your working hours. Therefore, setting clear boundaries is necessary to prevent distractions from hindering your progress.

In an ideal situation, you should have a dedicated office space in your house with a computer setup prepared exclusively for working. However, if you don't have a spare room, or the funds to buy a new computer, it is okay to create a temporary office in your bedroom with your personal setup.

However, it is common for family members to think that, since you are home, you are available to run some errands or perform household chores during the day. But that's not the case, when you work alone, your working hours are sacred: when you're not working, there is no one else pushing the project forward for you. Unless it is an emergency or something strictly necessary, any non-work related activity should be dealt with outside of your working hours.

Your family may not always understand what you do for a living, but it is important to set boundaries regarding your working hours. If possible, close the office door, so you can focus exclusively on your project. It may not seem like much, but even small interruptions are productivity killers. It disrupts your concentration and derails your train of thought. It may be difficult at the beginning, but most people are reasonable and will understand if you talk to them, and even if they don't, most people will notice you are actually working when the money starts entering your household.

Even though you may have flexible working hours, establishing a fixed routine will make it easier for family members to know when you are available. Following a routine is also beneficial for calibrating our brains for productivity. Personally, I like to follow the regional office hours standard: 8 to 5, with a 1-hour lunch break, Monday through Friday. This works for me, but you're free to organize your daily routine according to your most productive hours. Just keep in mind that you must follow your routine and put in the hours on your project, otherwise it will not move forward.

Pets should only be allowed in the office, if they do not become a distraction. For example, a dog or cat that just wants to take a nap next to you is okay, looking at them or petting them may even help reduce stress and anxiety. But if your pet is the type that jumps on the keyboard or is constantly seeking attention, it is better to keep them out of the office during working hours.

You must also avoid distracting yourself. Taking short breaks during the day is important, but during working hours, you must avoid productivity killers like checking on social media, playing video games, watching videos or TV shows, etc. Those are all activities that will consume hours before you notice.

Sure, some big tech companies offer leisure activities within the office and even claim that it helps increase productivity. But, in reality the 80/20 rule[13] also applies to productivity: usually 80% of the work is performed by the 20% of people that do not treat the work environment as kindergarten. Companies use leisure and recreational spaces as a hiring strategy, but are only able to maintain most of the workforce when the economy is booming or the market is in a financial bubble. That's why there are always massive layoffs in the tech industry from time to time. Whenever a financial crisis starts, big companies can safely get rid of most of the workforce without affecting productivity.

However, as a solo developer, you are the only one responsible for your project: distractions should be avoided like the plague! Leisure activities are important for your mental health, but they should be practiced in your spare time. If possible, it is recommended to have a computer exclusively for work, without any games installed and logged in only on work-related websites, as this will make it harder to access any distractions on this machine. Remember, even though you are working for yourself, in the comfort of your home, you must be professional and responsible with your time.

[13] Also known as the Pareto Principle

1.5.5. Wearing all the Hats

"Wearing all the hats" is a common expression used to describe someone that is responsible for multiple roles in a company. As an employee, being in this situation is only beneficial if your paycheck matches the amount of work and responsibility over your shoulders. But when you do have skin in the game[14], wearing all the hats at the early days of the business, may give you a valuable systemic vision of your company operation. As your company grows, you will have the basic knowledge to evaluate the work of others, like employees or freelancers. As an administrator, you don't have to know everything, but having basic knowledge of the key processes of your company is fundamental for making the right decisions. Even if you don't want to hire people and intend on remaining as a small one-person business, having a clear systemic vision of the business is fundamental for success.

Sure, wearing all the hats limits your productivity and may increase the risk of burnout. But doing so, at least on your first project, is a truly enriching experience. Even if you work alone, you don't have to wear all the hats forever. In future projects, you can delegate tasks you don't want to delve into to freelancers or external contractors. By having a basic understanding of the task you will not only be able to clearly describe what you need, but will also be able to evaluate if the results meet the initial requirements.

There's also a clear distinction between specialists and generalists in the job market. Specialists are capable of delivering higher levels of quality and solving issues faster, but only in a specific role. On the other hand, generalists are capable of delivering results within minimum quality requirements across a wide range of roles, making them more versatile. These differences have clear long-term implications, for example, specialists are more likely to be replaced by

---

[14] Someone that is financially invested in the company, usually the owner or a partner

robots or AI as technology evolves. Generalists, on the other hand, have an easier time adapting to market changes.

From a business perspective, doing everything by yourself gives you full control over the creative process. This is good for artists, but may be a limiting factor for entrepreneurs, as refusing to delegate tasks, may limit your company's growth potential. Some people do not mind continuing as a small one-person business for all their lives, and that is ok, as long as the revenue is enough to move on with your life. Others aspire to build a big company, in that case, delegating is inevitable. There is nothing wrong on either side, you are free to decide how high you want to climb your mountain.

As technology evolves, one-person businesses are also empowered to achieve higher productivity levels by leveraging the power of automation and generative tools. As I'm writing this book, AI generative tools are already a reality. Even though there is a big discussion regarding the moral implications of AI tools scraping content without consent on the internet, there are also people all over the world already using AI to lower costs of production and increase productivity. As we live in the early days of this new technology, there are still no regulations and there is plenty of uncertainty regarding the replacement of part of the workforce by these tools. Unfortunately, there are also people taking advantage of the unregulated market and flooding online stores with low quality 100% AI generated content. Maybe, these issues will be solved by future regulations, but even if it is not, many believe the Pandora Box[15] was open and there is no turning back.

I personally believe that AI is neither good or bad, it is just a tool, just like a knife, it can be used for good or evil, the result depends on the person wielding it. I also believe, that there is no way of creating good content without human interaction. Hopefully, in the future, AI tools may be used to automate and

[15] From the greek myth of Pandora

improve workflows in an ethical way, eliminating boring and repetitive tasks, but with humans having full control and still being responsible for the creative process. At least, that's what I hope for.

As for the influx of low quality generated content, low quality products are not sustainable in the long run. People tend to learn how to identify and boycott products like these. Negative reviews also help prevent more people from getting scammed, tainting the creator with a negative reputation. On the other hand, good quality content tends to accumulate positive reviews over time, building a good reputation for responsible and honest creators.

Considering a hypothetical future, in which AI is part of the workflow of every profession, honest creators will also be able to create good quality content faster. But that is only possible, by having a solid systemic vision of the project. I believe using AI will be very similar to hiring a freelancer: you can't get a good result if you don't know how to explain exactly what you need. By wearing all the hats at the start of your journey, you have a greater chance of developing the skills necessary to create high quality products, either alone or by delegating parts of the process to other people or machines.

1.5.6. Avoiding Stagnation

As a solo developer, you are solely responsible for planning which skills you should learn next. Otherwise, you risk professional stagnation. However, this problem is not unique to solo entrepreneurs: employees who stay in the same role for too long also have limited growth potential.

Most companies don't care about professional growth, even the ones that claim to. If someone has been performing the same function very well for a long time, it is beneficial for the company to keep them exactly where they are. After all, there is no need to replace a cog that is running smoothly.

For employees, this situation is bad from both a professional and financial perspective: by remaining in the same role, your salary most likely will remain the same. In the software development industry, programmers tend to avoid this situation, by applying for another position. This not only opens up the possibility of working with new technologies, but it also creates an opportunity to negotiate a higher salary as compensation for leaving your current job.

But, how can solo entrepreneurs avoid this issue? Well, the answer lies in your product catalog. At the start of your journey, focus on learning skills to improve your workflow efficiency and the quality of your products. If you have the means for it, don't be afraid to invest in good tools and courses related to your craft. At this stage, building a strong foundation should be your top priority.

As your catalog grows, stagnation can be avoided by exploring different product genres within your market. On top of the learning benefits, this exploratory phase also increases your chances of finding profitable product niches. This stage is about leveraging the foundations you've built to expand your knowledge and your reach within your market.

Once your first product catalog is well established, it's a good time to diversify your revenue streams, perhaps by creating a secondary product catalog on another marketplace or even exploring a completely new market. This not only forces you to learn something new, but also prevents you from having all the eggs in a single basket. At this stage, be careful to not neglect your primary source of revenue[16]. The idea is to diversify revenue streams, not replace them.

Multiple revenue streams act as a safety net. If one of your revenue streams is affected by external factors, you can still rely on the others while taking action to mitigate the situation. It's the same diversification strategy used in the financial market, but applied from a business perspective.

[16] Even solid foundations need maintenance from time to time.

1.5.7. Finding New Ideas

Brainstorming can be defined as the process of leveraging the collective wisdom of a group of people to tackle a problem from multiple perspectives. When applied correctly, it can be a powerful problem solving and decision making technique. However, as a solo developer, you are limited to your own perspective, so it is necessary to workaround this limitation.

When looking for a solution, the first thing you should do is research. The world is a big place, there is a great chance someone, somewhere, had the same problem before. Contrary to popular belief, good problem solvers aren't geniuses that create a new solution on the fly for everything. For most problems, there is no need to reinvent the wheel, specially tech related problems, if you know how and where to look, you'll probably find multiple solutions scattered around internet forums, if you're lucky, you may even find detailed step-by-step guides on how to solve it.

Therefore, learning how to properly search for a solution is the first step to becoming a good problem solver. If there is an error message, just copy and paste it on the search bar and you will be amazed at how fast you can find a solution. If not, try to break down the problem, by identifying "where", "how" and "when" the problem manifests itself, and use this information to build your search queries. For example, does it happen on a specific tool? What happens when the issue occurs? What triggers it to happen? What was the last action you took before it happened? Etc. By learning how to ask the right questions, you'll be one step closer to solving any issues.

If, for some reason, you are unable to find a solution, or if you are designing a product to solve a previously unresolved issue. Now is the time to reach for the drawing board, but it is important to only do this after the research phase. Since you don't have any teammates, you need to open your mind and make a list of all possible solutions you can think of. At this stage, don't leave any idea out of the list, write every single one of them, no matter how stupid or simple they may seem. It is important to make an effort to look at the problem from different angles. It is harder to do this alone, but it gets easier over time. After finishing the list, rearrange all possible solutions in order of complexity. Simple solutions have higher priority, so you should try them first, you should only try complex solutions if none of the simple ones works. Remember, the same problem may have multiple solutions, but complex solutions always consume more time and resources, therefore simple solutions are always better.

If you are looking for ideas for your next product, instead of trying to imagine something new and disruptive, it is easier to look for problems and then develop a solution for them. People are not always inclined to try something new, but are always happy to purchase something that eliminates a problem.

1.5.8. Getting Feedback

Feedback is an essential part of the growth cycle. After all, it's impossible to improve if you don't know what's wrong. However, sometimes it's difficult to acknowledge your own mistakes. As part of a team, you can receive feedback from your colleagues and supervisors. But where do you find feedback when you are working alone? The answer is quite simple, you get it the same way companies do: from the market.

Paying customers are the most valuable source of feedback you can possibly have. Since they are financially invested into your product, they have a really good reason to report issues and make improvement suggestions. Clients may not understand the tech behind the product, but addressing their needs is what drives business growth.

For technical and business related feedback, you need the opinion of professionals. That's harder to find, which is why networking is so important. Do you have friends or contacts who work in the same market? Is there a local group or association related to your field? If so, are there events or meetings? Are there online groups or communities? Knowing other professionals and entrepreneurs from your field is indispensable for understanding the market you are stepping in. Not everyone is a competitor, there are people truly interested in sharing information for mutual benefit. The best professionals do not withhold knowledge, on the contrary, they evolve by teaching and learning from others.

Just be aware of phonies and scammers, especially fake internet gurus. It is wise to only take advice from people who actually accomplished what they are teaching. If you are looking for business advice, you must listen to businessmen that are more successful than you. If you are looking for a technical opinion, you should look for more experienced professionals. Whenever you are the most experienced person in the room, give back to those who humbly seek your help.

When attending networking events, it is essential to maintain professional etiquette. If you don't know those around you, simply listen and observe before speaking, you'll be surprised at how effective this is in avoiding unnecessary conflict. Always be humble and respectful to everyone, and avoid people who are not. Humility is a sign of honesty and believe me, mutual cooperation is only possible between honest people. You must surround yourself with positive influences only. This is how you build meaningful and valuable connections.

1.5.9. Motivation & Consistency

Ideally, you should be able to focus on your goals and use that as motivation to keep moving forward. Most fake gurus "teach" people that visualizing your future success and believing in yourself is all it takes to become an "overnight millionaire". And when that obviously doesn't work, they claim you simply didn't try hard enough or didn't follow their "secret protocol" correctly. I hate to be the bearer of bad news, but there are no secret formulas for success nor a guaranteed way to always feel motivated.

Real life is not that simple, in a world filled with distractions and hardships along the way, most people struggle with motivation and self-discipline. However, most people are also able to consistently attend to a job they hate for an entire lifetime. So, what is the catch? If they are not motivated to go to work, why do they do it anyway? Well, the answer is actually really simple, you don't need motivation to move forward: you need consistency. Most days you'll not feel motivated or inspired, but you need to get out of the bed and do it anyway.

Motivation is a positive feeling that boosts your productivity, but it is impossible to only experience positive feelings all the time, so it is necessary to learn how to be productive even on the bad days. The world is a harsh place, most people are broken, bad days and negative feelings are more common than good ones, so you can't rely on good days to be productive. Since bad days are inevitable, learning how to harvest negative emotions and converting them into power is essential to be a functional adult.

And that brings us to the answer on why people attend jobs they hate. The answer is fear, the fear of starvation, the fear of becoming homeless if you don't pay your bills and the fear of not being able to provide for your family. It is pure survival instinct, the same way our ancestors left the cave to hunt for prey, nowadays people leave their houses to hunt for a paycheck. Most people don't have the luxury of having a support network, so they have no choice other than keep pushing forward.

The thing is, regardless if you are going to work on a regular job that you hate or if you are gonna be your own boss, you're going to have to work anyway. You just need to decide if you're gonna work for the safety of a fixed paycheck or to build a better future for yourself.

Your career is just like a marathon towards your goals. The only difference is that failure is behind you, getting closer and closer, so you can't stop moving. If focusing on the finishing line is enough to get you motivated, good, keep going. But, if that's not enough, try looking back over your shoulder and face what is coming to get you if you fail, maybe that will push you forward. Just don't panic, it is not a sprint race, it is a marathon. It is ok to sprint from time to time, but if you do it all the time you are going to burnout. Slow and steady is enough to keep momentum. The important thing is to keep moving forward.

Fear is not the only negative emotion that can be harvested for motivation, hate is also a very powerful emotion. When I left my job to become an entrepreneur in the games industry, it took me over a year to start making enough money to stop burning through my savings. It was really hard to get up everyday and keep working for months in a row without any financial compensation, but when things got harsh, I used to look back and remember how much I hated working as someone else's employee. I have burned that hatred as fuel, day after day, to power through those tough times. To be honest, I'm not sure if that's healthy or not, but if the hounds of hell are out there to get us no matter what, why not trick them and strap them in the front of the wagon?

1.6. Solo Development Workflow

When it comes to project management, big companies have tools, processes and best practices designed to deal with large teams. As a solo developer, you don't need excessive bureaucracy, but also can't afford to be sloppy. You have limited time and resources that need to be organized and properly managed, otherwise you won't be able to finish your project. The best case scenario, is to follow a lean and optimized workflow[17] for both business and project management.

An optimized workflow, has the minimum amount of steps necessary to complete a task or project, without sacrificing the minimum quality requirements. Ideally, it must be a cyclical process that produces value on each iteration. It must also be well defined and documented, so it can be easily reproduced or even taught to others. In this regard, simplicity is key, complexity doesn't make things better, it only makes them harder to develop and maintain. That's why I have decided to adopt simplified workflows to handle both the administrative and technical aspects of my business.

1.6.1. Simplified Business Management

From a macro perspective, a business operation can be simplified into three phases: Planning, Execution & Monitoring.

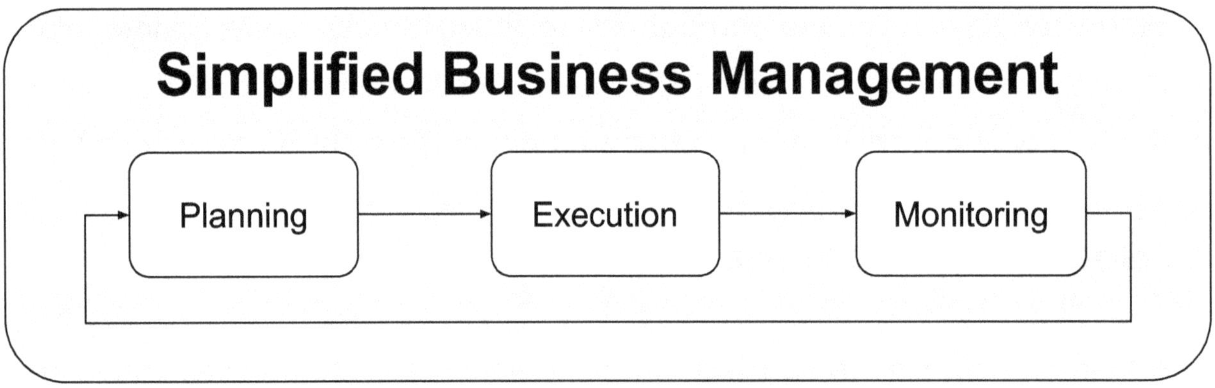

Figure: Simplified Business Management

Planning is essential to increase your chances of success, creating a business plan may seem like unnecessary bureaucracy for solo developers, but in reality, human memory is not reliable, if you do not transfer your ideas to paper,

[17] Workflow can be defined as a sequence of activities or steps needed to complete a specific task or project. Think of it like a step-by-step guide on how to achieve a specific goal. For example, a step-by-step guide on how to perform an operation is a workflow for that specific task, the day-to-day routine of an employee can be interpreted as that role workflow.

they may get lost and so do you. A business plan serves as a beacon of light that guides you towards your goals, it is like a map that shows you the way, the dangers and opportunities ahead. A well defined business plan, allows you to have a systemic vision of your business and its long term financial feasibility. It gives you a clear idea of whether or not your idea is worth pursuing. I know, paperwork is boring, especially for creative individuals, but if you plan on making a living as a solo developer, it is unwise to ignore this step.

Since the focus of this book is project management, I won't get into details on how to make a business plan. Business plan models are easily accessible on the internet, my only recommendation is to keep it simple. Unless you're planning on getting a loan to start your business, you don't need a highly detailed business plan. As a solo developer starting a small operation, you may not need a loan, you may use your own funds or start your business as a side hustle. A simplified business plan is a guide for you, it only needs to contain information relevant for your business, like your goals, strategy, operation plan, competitors, distribution channels, potential clients, marketing plan, etc. The idea is not to create a massive document that you'll never read again, it is to create a guide for your business that you can revisit as many times as you need to remember where you're going and how you plan to get there.

Execution is the business operation, that's when the strategy defined on the business plan is put to practice. For developers, that's where the projects are created, alongside any other day-to-day activity related to your business.

And last, but not least, the monitoring phase, which is essentially comparing your results with your initial goals. Are you moving forward? Is your strategy effective? What went wrong? What went right? Etc. Looking back and analyzing your progress, gives you the opportunity to adapt your strategy before starting the next production cycle. Ideally, this should be done in between projects, to identify improvement points on your production workflow, and at least once a year to track your business progress. But in order to do that, you need to gather data, for example, you may keep track of how many units were sold and how much revenue was generated by each product. That way, you can identify which products in your portfolio have higher potential[18].

Once the monitoring phase is complete, it is time to go back to your business plan, document your current progress and any changes made on your strategy. Do not edit the previous business plan, create a new copy and keep track of the creation date, that way, you will also have a history of your business strategy evolution. You don't need to update your business plan after finishing each project, especially when your strategy consists of releasing multiple small products, but it is recommended to update it at least once a year. Keep in mind that, even though monitoring is at the end of the business management cycle, data collection should be a parallel task, included in your daily routine.

By iterating through these three phases (planning, execution and monitoring)[19] you'll be doing the least amount of work necessary to keep your business alive.

1.6.2. Simplified Project Management

One of the main reasons solo developers fail to complete projects is completely neglecting project management. It is common for beginners to have an idea and start developing right away, without any planning or deeper consideration about the project's feasibility. This may work for micro project's, that may be complete in a day or two, but anything bigger than that, is prone to

---

[18] Tracking your sales is the bare minimum you need to analyze your business progress. You may also track other aspects of your business as it grows, like productivity, customer satisfaction, etc. Every important information is considered a key performance indicator (also known as KPIs)

[19] These phases cover only the functional aspects of a business operation, any other business related bureaucracy, for example, legal and fiscal obligations should be delegated to an accountant.

fail without proper planning. As mentioned before, excessive bureaucracy is also not required and may even be detrimental to solo developers. Therefore, adopting a simplified project management strategy is the best case scenario.

Project management is basically breaking down the project into smaller tasks, these tasks are then organized, prioritized, delegated[20] and monitored. It is very similar to task management, however, it also involves managing the time and resources available to make sure the project is completed. For solo developers, it all boils down to having a small and well defined project scope and keeping track of your project progress throughout its lifecycle.

Nowadays, there are free project management platforms, which includes task, time and team management tools. In chapter 2, I'll show some examples on how to use one of these tools for planning and keeping track of your project.

1.6.3. Simplified Development Cycle

Managing your business and project is crucial, but it won't matter if you don't know how to execute your project. Since solo developers usually operate with limited resources, adopting a simplified and optimized workflow is part of a good project management strategy. The first step is to understand the development cycle of your product. For software related projects, it can be simplified into four phases: Planning, Development, Release & Support.

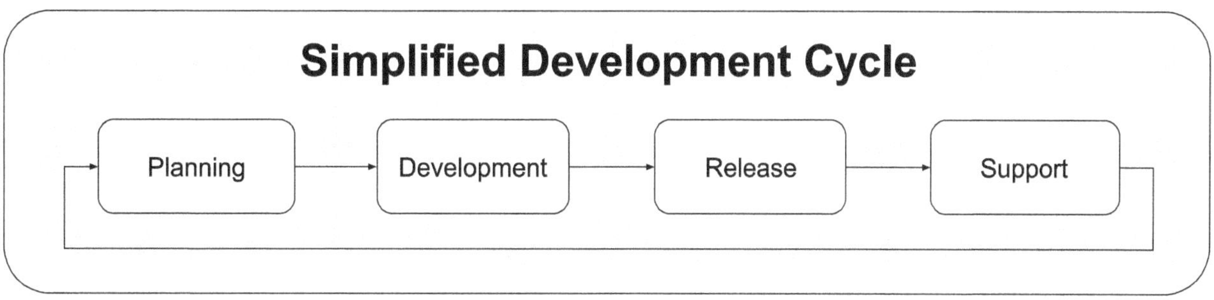

Figure: Simplified Development Cycle

[20] Solo developers may delegate tasks to freelancers or skip this step and assume every task

Every new product, or product update, is an iteration of this cycle. In the following chapters, I'll break down every phase in detail and give some tips and tricks on how to organize yourself and keep track of your progress as you go.

Chapter 2: Project Planning

The first phase of a project, the main objectives of this stage are: validating feasibility, delimiting the project scope and creating a design document to serve as a guide in the development process.

2.1. Product Design

Product design is the art of creating desirable products. Have you ever wondered why people acquire non-essential products? What makes them valuable or desirable? These products sell because they are either useful or appealing. The first step to validate your project feasibility is to ask yourself: Why would someone pay for this? Is it useful? If not, is it at least appealing?

By creating a product that is both useful and appealing, you'll have greater chances of success. However, as a beginner, it may be easier to focus on what is easier for you to achieve based on your background. For example, as a programmer it is easier for me to create something useful, on the other hand, artists will find it easier to create something appealing.

As a rule of thumb, when looking for ideas for your next project, rather than trying to come up with a new and disruptive product that will revolutionize the world, it's easier to look for pain points in the market and focus on finding potential solutions. Of course, innovation is important, but it's harder to convince people to adopt something new than selling a solution to an existing problem. If your product is a solution, it's useful and therefore desirable.

2.1.1. Market Research

Once you have a clear idea of what you want to build, the second step for validating the project's feasibility is to analyze the market. The main goal of this stage is to identify your potential customers and competitors.

One of the benefits of creating solutions is having a clear vision of your target audience. If you can find people complaining about the issue you're trying to solve, then you know where to focus your marketing efforts. It doesn't have to be a complex problem, as long as a large number of people are affected by it, even a solution for a simple problem has the potential to be profitable.

It's also important to look for competitors. Is anyone selling something similar? If not, maybe this is your lucky day. When you are the first one selling a solution, you have the opportunity of dominating the early days of the market niche, which is not only highly profitable, but also increases your chances of becoming the biggest player in that niche, provided, of course, that your solution is accepted by the market. However, if you encounter competitors, don't be discouraged: there's nothing wrong with wanting a share of the market.

If you do have competitors, you may as well use any information you may acquire about them to your advantage, as long as you play fair, there is nothing wrong with it. Starting from the obvious, if someone is already selling a similar product, this means it is possible to make money from it. It also means, you don't have to start from scratch, you can list your most successful competitors and analyze what they have in common. That way, you can identify which features your version of the product needs, in order to match the most successful competitors. It is also recommended to analyze customer feedback, to identify improvement points and avoid any mistakes made by your predecessors.

Another benefit of having competitors is having information about pricing. This information is key for project feasibility analysis. Does the average price match the amount of effort necessary to create this project? If not, it is better to pursue something else. If you decide on following through with the project, you will also be able to properly price your product, by making a simple qualitative comparison with similar products.

Overpricing and underpricing should be avoided. If you are able to deliver a better product, or at least the same quality level, at a similar price range, you'll have greater chances of receiving your fair share of the market. Of course, there are some exceptions: if your product is better, you may charge more, if it is worse you may charge less, but be aware that having a huge price gap between you and your competitors has negative impacts. If your product is too expensive, customers won't buy it, but if it is too cheap, they may think it lacks quality[21]. By underpricing your product, you are also undermining your professional value, this is prejudicial not only for you, but for the market as a whole.

2.1.2. Marketplace Guidelines

If you intend on publishing your product on a third-party marketplace, you must be aware of the marketplace guidelines. Marketplaces may have restrictions on the allowed type of products, among other details that need to be taken in consideration during product design, to prevent it from being rejected or taken down from the store. Do not neglect the marketplace guidelines, otherwise you risk wasting time creating a product that will not be approved for publishing.

2.1.3. User Experience

User experience, also known as UX, refers to the product usability, accessibility and overall feel. A product may be useful, but if it is not user-friendly, it may be rejected by the target audience.

[21] The target audience's consumer habits also affect the optimal pricing range.

Ideally, a product should be as easy as possible to use. It doesn't matter if your target audience is a niche of highly qualified professionals, any complexity should be hidden away behind a user-friendly interface. The easier it is to use, the higher its chances of receiving positive reviews, which in return, makes it easier to reach more clients, creating a snowball effect that maximizes organic reach.

The visual appeal of your product also contributes to a good user experience. However, if you manage to create something that is both useful and user-friendly, you already have a solid and functional product. Of course, making it also visually appealing will increase your chances of reaching more clients, so this should not be neglected either[22].

2.2. Project Scope

The project scope is a clear delimitation of what features must be included in the project. From the technical perspective, this is the most important product design concept, as the number one reason solo developers are unable to finish what they've started is not having a well defined project scope. The common mistakes made by solo developers are: defining a massive scope, expanding the scope before finishing the project or having no defined scope at all. Luckily, there is a solo development friendly strategy that will help you create a properly sized and realistic project scope: the MVP strategy.

MVP stands for Minimum Viable Product, this strategy consists of launching a product that includes only the strictly necessary features, then gradually improving it through updates based on customer feedback. At first glance, it may seem a little shady to use early adopters to validate your product, but when implemented correctly, this strategy is a win-win situation for both sides.

---

[22] If you're aiming for usability, visual appeal is the cherry on the top. However, some niches revolve entirely around visual appeal, so it depends on what you are trying to build.

For the developer, the main benefit is being able to gather feedback directly from the market as soon as possible, this makes it easier to test multiple product ideas and focus only on the good ones. After all, it is better to release multiple small products and let clients decide which ones have potential, then spend a lot of time and resources developing something big, that you don't even know if it will be accepted by the market.

For clients, the main benefit is being able to tailor the product to match their needs. Think of this, how many big companies completely ignore client feedback? How many times have you been frustrated with a product that does almost everything you need, but lacks fundamental features? Being heard and having a product you own improved based on your suggestions, not only makes it more useful for you, but also makes your investment worth the price. Clients are far more likely to be satisfied and leave a positive review on a product they've helped improve. When a client suggestion is implemented, it creates a meaningful connection between the client and the product and there is nothing more powerful than that for earning customer loyalty.

Here is how to implement this strategy. The first step to define a MVP scope, is to make a list of all relevant features, at this stage do not leave any feature idea out of the list, including features that may only be included on future updates. If you have competitors, it is recommended to use the most successful similar products as reference to build the feature list, this will save you a lot of time and facilitate your brainstorming session. Once the features list is complete, sort it by relevance and select only fundamental features as part of the initial scope. The goal is for the first version to have the least amount of features necessary to make the product functional. Any other optional features or possible improvements, should be kept as a roadmap for future versions. Remember, you are still not sure if those features are necessary or desired by the clients, so it is risky to waste time on them at this stage.

After the first release, if the product sparks the interest of the public, you'll start receiving suggestions and bug reports. Suggestions that make sense within the product context, should be added to the features roadmap, minor bugs may also be treated the same way. However, any critical bugs should be given top priority and fixed as soon as possible through patches or hotfixes[23], especially in the early days of the product life cycle. Ideally, any product should be stable and bug free on release, but even though it is possible to minimize the risk of a critical bug reaching the market, it is impossible to guarantee it may not happen. If it does, the faster you handle the situation and deploy the fix, the greater your chances of reverting any possible negative reviews.

Once you have gathered enough feedback for the next update, use the roadmap as reference to define the scope of the next iteration of the product. The goal is to fix all bugs from the previous version and add the most requested features. Every new iteration makes the product more robust and complete, increasing its chances of success.

In summary, that's how the MVP strategy works, the first version of the product serves as a prototype to be validated by the market. A MVP product is considered a success, when it is able to generate revenue and spark the interest of the public. If it doesn't, move on and start developing your next MVP. The idea is to always work on small development cycles, as you gradually expand and improve your product catalog.

2.2.1. Task Management

Once the project scope is defined, the next step is to break it into smaller pieces to facilitate task management and execution. From a systemic perspective, task management consists of keeping track of all activities that need to be executed in order to complete the project.

[23] A hotfix is an urgent update, deployed as soon as possible to solve a critical issue

The base minimum you need to keep track is: task name, description and status. But, you may also track additional information, like assigned team members, deadline, start and end dates, priority, etc. It all depends on how much you want to simplify or detail your task management workflow.

Personally, I prefer board-based task management solutions[24], as they are easy to use, highly customizable and makes it easier to have an overall vision of the project progress. There are several task management tools available, which one you choose is just a matter of preference.

Boards are fairly simple, they are composed of columns and cards, which may represent whatever you heart desire. Cards are grouped into columns and may be rearranged in any order or moved to other columns. Within a project management context, cards can be used to represent single tasks, while columns represent the task current status. For example, a project board may be divided into the following three columns: *Backlog*, *In Progress* and *Completed*.

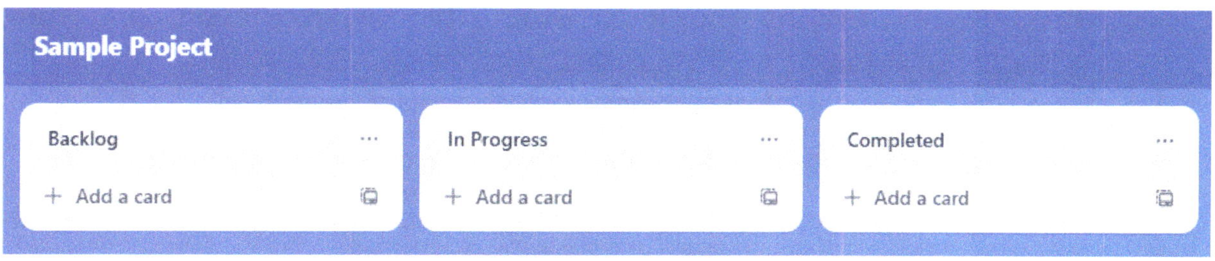

Figure: Sample Task Management Board

In the backlog column, add a new task for every feature listed in the project scope. However, keep in mind that tasks and features are not equivalent. Features are broad descriptions of functionalities, and even though simple features may be listed as a single task, complex features are usually divided into multiple tasks that may or may not be executed by the same person.

[24] The following samples were created using https://trello.com/

For the task name, it is recommended to use the following naming convention: "version number - short task description." This naming convention makes it easier to track what was included in each project iteration. Note that the three-digit software versioning standard was used in this example. From left to right, the digits correspond to: major update, minor update, and patch number (e.g., v1.0.0).

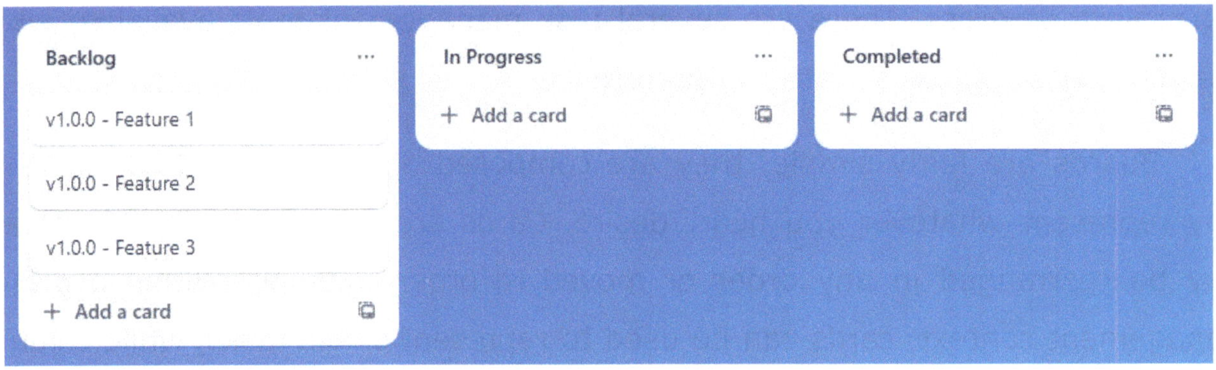

Figure: Backlog Sample

The backlog list is complete, once all features of the project scope are included. It is highly recommended to order the backlog tasks in order of execution, as this will facilitate the next steps.

As you start working on a task, move it from the Backlog to the "In Progress" column. Adding an expected deadline is recommended to avoid getting too comfortable, it serves as a psychological finish line to prevent procrastination.

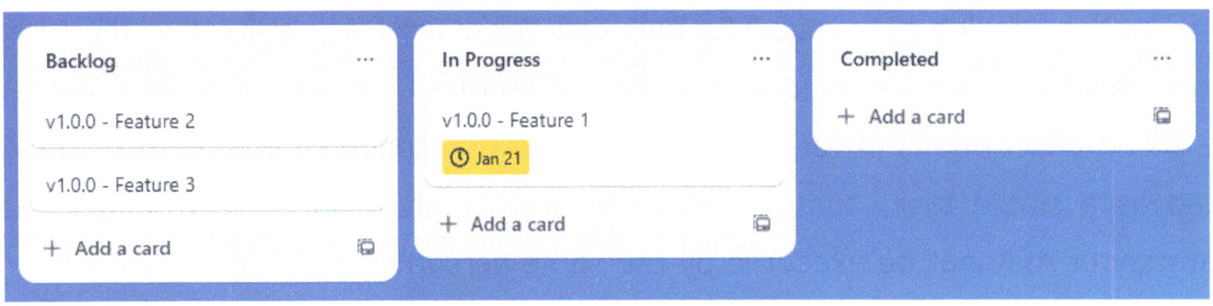

Figure: Task In Progress

Once a task is completed, set its end date to keep track of your progress and move it to the top of the next column. Repeat the cycle for the next task, the goal is to move all tasks from left to right.

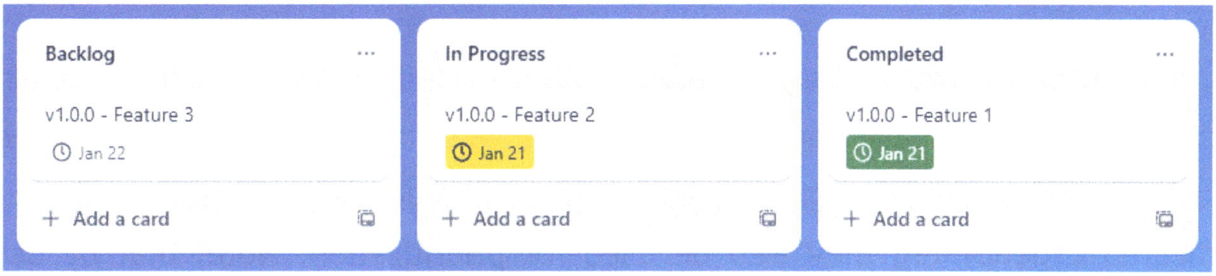

Figure: Completed Task Sample

After finishing the project, the backlog column can be used as a roadmap for future versions, as you gather feedback from the market. By using the recommended naming convention, you may even plan ahead and schedule features to specific versions. In the following example, some suggestions and minor bugs were scheduled for the first minor update (v1.1.0).

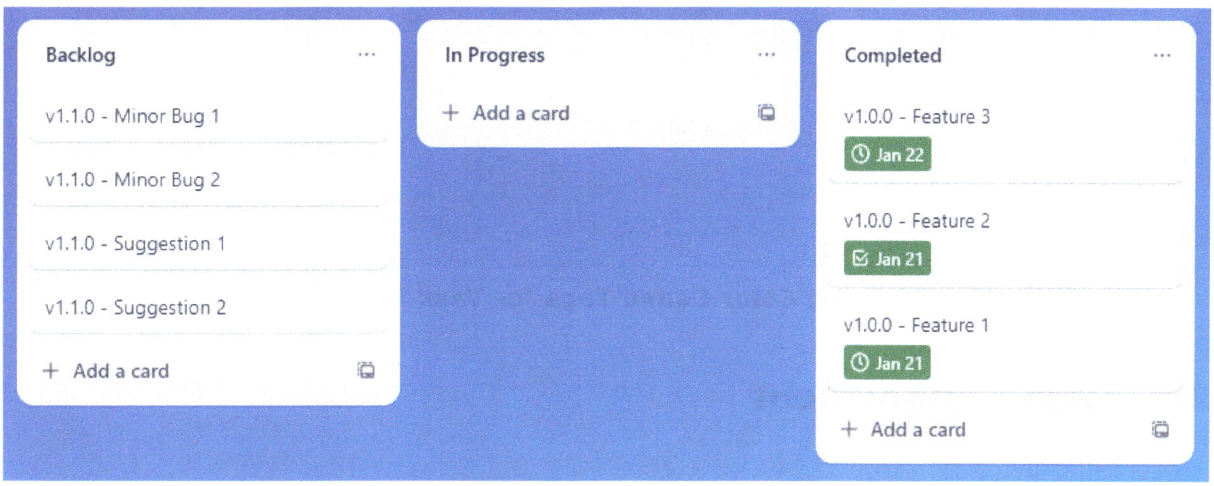

Figure: Adding the Roadmap to the Backlog

This simplified task management workflow is perfectly fit for solo developers. It is simple, easy to follow and a really powerful organization tool. It not only prevents you from getting lost, but also serves as a motivation, every time you complete a new task you are rewarded with the feeling of moving forward. Perceiving your progress on every step has a powerful psychological effect, that will help remaining focused on your goals.

2.2.2. Task Prioritization

Another benefit of using a digital board-based solution, is being able to easily reorder tasks based on priority. Using a color coded tag system is also very effective. For example, tags can be used to categorize bugs and features. A dedicated urgency tag may also be used for prioritization. Note, that by using three simple tags, the board has become far more readable and intuitive.

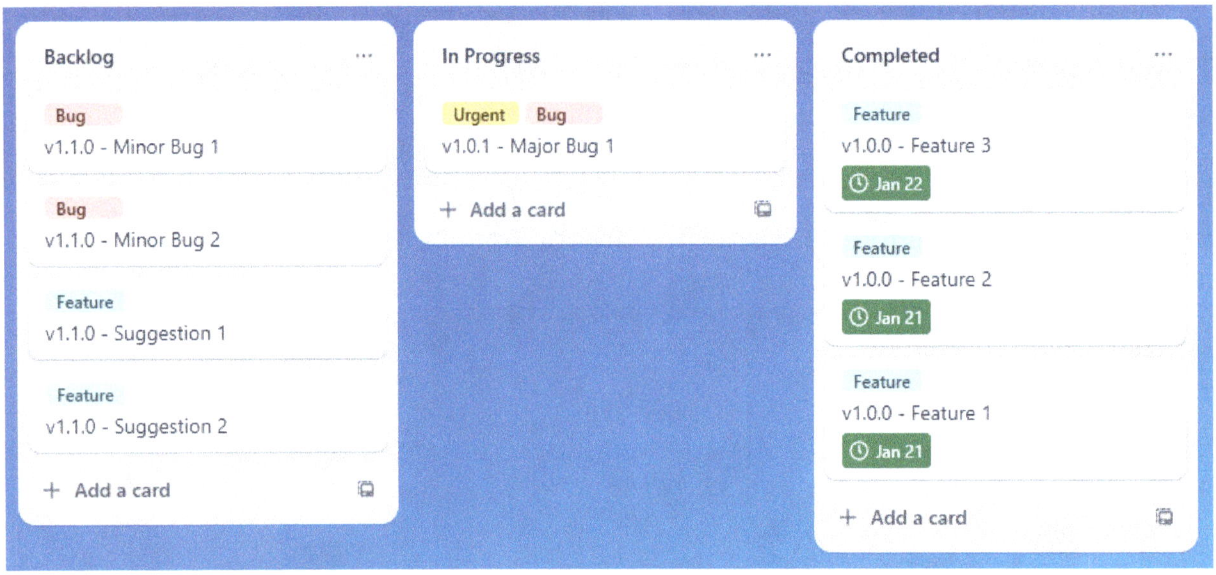

Figure: Using Color Coded Tags for Task Prioritization

2.2.3. Time Management

It's time to talk about a topic feared by solo developers: deadlines. If you are a hobbyist, you can take your time and enjoy the process, but for entrepreneurs, deadlines are a necessary evil. While they may be stressful and it's very difficult to predict how long it will take to finish a specific task, the lack of a deadline increases the chances of procrastination.

You don't have to know exactly when you're gonna start and finish each task, as this is virtually impossible, but having at least a deadline for finishing the project will help you avoid getting sloppy. Setting a deadline for a task when it is taken from the backlog is also a good strategy to manage your time, as it is easier to estimate one task at a time than to estimate the entire backlog.

If you want to go a step further, you can also estimate tasks weekly. For example, on Monday morning, set deadlines for all the tasks you believe you can complete that week. By having a weekly schedule, your chances of making progress that week increase exponentially. If you can't finish everything on time, simply reschedule the overdue tasks and move on. Missing a deadline is awful, but it's not the end of the world. As you become more experienced, you'll get better at estimating deadlines for tasks you've already completed, and even then, you may still miss some deadlines for unexpected reasons beyond your control. That's life, you just have to learn to live with it.

2.3. Technical Research

Software development basically consists of converting real-world concepts and processes into virtual solutions. The official computer science term for this process is: abstraction. Since most software are abstractions of the real world, on top of having technical knowledge about programming, software developers are also required to delve into any other technical field, understand the key concepts and extract any information that is relevant to the context of the application. In the software development industry, the technical research is usually conducted by a software architect, during the project planning phase. However, as a solo developer, you'll be responsible for both planning and execution.

Technical books, academic papers, articles, technical documentation, etc. It doesn't matter where you get your information, as long as it is accurate and relevant to your project. Remember, the goal is not to become an expert, it is to gather the minimum amount of information necessary to execute the project. For example, if the project consists of a flight simulation game, there is no need to deep dive on aeronautical engineering, but knowing the basics principles of plane physics is definitely going to make a difference.

Once the project scope and technical research are completed, they can be used to identify which tools and technologies are better suited for the project. For example, for a software related project, this would consist of which programming languages and Design Patterns[25] are going to be used, alongside with any other tools and services required.

2.4. Design Document

At the end of the project planning phase, it is recommended to create a Design Document with all relevant technical information about the project. This includes the project scope, tools and technologies, and any other information about the project architecture.

Unfortunately, documentation is a tedious and time-consuming process, often neglected by developers, even on big companies. However, if the project is successful and the development team eventually needs to be expanded, having technical documentation will reduce the time and effort required to train new team members. Furthermore, the design document serves as a technical guide during development, as it is essentially a blueprint of the project.

---

[25] Design Patterns are commonly used project structures used as base for software development.

Chapter 3: Development Phase

Now is the moment of truth, it is time to execute your project. If you've come this far, be proud of yourself and try to enjoy the process as much as possible. This is the hardest part of the journey, but also the most rewarding, as most of the learning opportunities are at this stage.

3.1. Sharpening the Axe

If you are already experienced with the tools and technologies required by the project, you may skip the step and head straight to execution. However, in the software development industry, being required to learn new tools or technologies for a specific project is fairly common, even for experienced developers. If you find yourself in this situation, you may start by accessing the official documentation, as some tools are well documented and have practical examples for getting started.

However, if you have a hard time learning from the documentation, then it is recommended to look for a beginners course. Nowadays, tech courses and tutorials are easily accessible through the internet. My recommendation is to look for short duration courses, focused on the specific technologies you need to learn. That way, you avoid losing time learning things you won't need for your project[26].

For paid courses, it is recommended to only trust platforms that have a reliable review system, so you can attest the course quality before investing. If you don't find any free courses or tutorials, don't be afraid of investing in paid courses. Some skills are more than worth paying for, anything you can learn once and use to make money later must be considered an investment.

[26] "Learning under demand" is more effective than following trends and trying to learn everything.

Completing a good beginners course will give you the basic knowledge you need for starting your project. In the future, you may enroll in an intermediate or advanced course to sharpen your skills even further, but for starting a project, the basic skill level is enough, for a very specific reason: technical skills improve faster when put into practice. If you learn the basics and put it into practice right away, you will eventually reach the intermediate skill level on your own. Putting your new skills into practice as soon as possible will prevent you from getting stuck in "Tutorial Hell"[27]. Once you have mastered the basics of the tools and technologies required for the project, it is time to start execution.

3.2. Preparing the Development Environment

The first step of the development phase is preparing the development environment. This process consists of installing, setting up, and testing all tools necessary for the project. Depending on how complex your project is, this process could take an entire day, sometimes even more.

3.2.1. Version Control & Backups

Once the development environment is ready, it is time to open the development tools and create your project. However, before implementing the first feature, it is important to properly safeguard your progress. In the software development industry, this is done by using a Version Control System.

Version Control is the ultimate backup solution, it allows project members to access the most recent version of the project, make contributions, and solve any possible conflicts. It saves a history of all changes made to the project, so if any major mistake is made, it is possible to revert back to a previous version.

---

[27] "Tutorial Hell" is a term used to refer to beginners that get stuck watching tutorials, one after the other, and lose precious time learning stuff they will never use, instead of putting what they've learned into practice.

Even though solo developers don't have to worry about solving conflicts, it is good practice to use version control instead of relying on manual backups. By versioning the changes made on your project at the end of the day, you minimize the risk of losing your progress. Life is unpredictable, you never know when your computer may stop working. There are several version control solutions available, most of which are cloud based and offer free licensing tiers. You may pick whichever is more suitable for your project.

3.3. Developing the Main Features

If you've followed all the recommendations so far, congratulations! You're ready to start your project. At this point, you have a clear vision of what you want to build, the project scope is defined, and the tasks are organized in order of priority in the backlog. Now, you just need to follow the workflow defined in the task management section: one after the other, tasks should be removed from the backlog, executed, and marked as complete.

The backlog is your step-by-step guide on how to complete your project: each completed task is a new step toward your goal. Just keep moving forward, and eventually, you'll reach the finish line.

3.3.1. How to Avoid Development Hell

"Stuck in Development Hell" is a common expression for projects that get stuck in the development phase for a long time. From large companies to individual developers, this problem can affect any project, and the main reason for it is the lack of planning and organization. Fortunately, this situation can be avoided by following some best practices:

- **Do not skip the project planning phase:** Planning and preparing reduces your chances of getting lost.

- **The Project Scope should be realistic:** Large projects require large teams, solo developers should prefer small projects.
- **Do not expand the project scope mid project:** The first version should contain only MVP features. New feature ideas should be added to the roadmap of future versions.
- **Do not neglect task management:** The backlog is a step-by-step guide on how to finish your project. If you don't list the pending tasks, you won't know what to do next and will get lost.
- **Break big problems into smaller pieces:** Most complex problems are just a series of simple concepts put together. If you get stuck on a specific task, there is a great chance it is too big to be handled all at once. Try breaking it into smaller tasks, and then handle them sequentially.
- **Leverage momentum:** Avoid pausing projects to work on something else. Getting back to a project requires a lot of extra effort analysing what is already done and how it connects to what still needs to be done.
- **Maintain focus:** Avoid parallel development cycles. Working on multiple projects at the same time won't make you more productive, it will only make the projects take longer to be finished. Instead of releasing two products a year from now, it is better to release a product every six months. By the time the second product is released, the first one already has six months of accumulated revenue.
- **Close technical gaps:** If you lack the technical skills to solve a specific task, consider learning those skills. Learning under demand is part of the daily routine of a problem solver.

3.3.2. Devlogs

Once the project reaches the point of maturity in which it is possible to showcase some features, you may consider posting regular devlogs[28] to gather the attention of potential clients. The idea is to gather a community of people around the project, to increase the product sales on day one. This strategy also raises brand awareness, potentially increasing sales of future releases in the long run. Sure, devlogs do take time from the development phase, some developers make simple posts, with screenshots or GIF's showcasing the features, others create long videos with detailed explanations. In the end, how much effort you wish to invest on devlogs is up to you.

3.4. Testing Phase

As the project progresses, it is natural to identify bugs and issues along the way. As frustrating as it can be, dealing with these issues is part of the process. Minor bugs can be added on the backlog, to be dealt with after implementing all pending features. However, any issues that hinders the progress of the project, by preventing the execution of a task, should be dealt with immediately.

Once all features are completed, the project enters the "polishing stage", also known as alpha stage, which consists of eliminating all remaining bugs and issues, to make sure the product is stable for release. Since MVP projects usually don't have beta testing[29], it is important to thoroughly test every feature to minimize the chances of a major bug reaching the market.

Automated testing tools may also be used to ensure the quality and reliability of the application, especially when the same test needs to be performed

[28] Regular posts showcasing the progress of a project

[29] Alpha testing is an internal process conducted by the developers, beta testing is conducted by members of the target audience.

multiple times. For example, automated tests can be created to validate if the main features are still working correctly, after changes were made to the application. Keep in mind that automated tests do not eliminate the need for manual testing. Depending on the situation and the size of the application, manual testing may be faster than writing automated tests. However, as the application grows, the complexity of the test case scenarios increases exponentially, therefore, test automation is necessary to guarantee your testing capabilities scales at the same proportion.

3.4.1. Known Issues & Troubleshootings

Consider the following situations:

- Issues that cannot be solved due to current technological limitations.
- Issues that are caused by bugs on third-party related software.
- Compatible third-party software with confusing integration workflows.

Issues like these may be identified on the testing stage, but due to external factors, cannot be solved at the moment. However, even though your hands are tied, these situations cannot be neglected, as they have the potential of generating recurring support requests.

As a palliative solution, issues like this can be documented as known issues, to make it easier to handle related support requests. Within the task management workflow, any issues that fall in this situation, can be categorized and documented as troubleshootings[30]. Here is a practical example:

[30] The reason I prefer the term "Troubleshooting" over "Known Issues" is that it can also be used to document internal issues. For example, if one of the tools used in the project has a confusing workflow, this can also be documented as a troubleshooting solution for future reference.

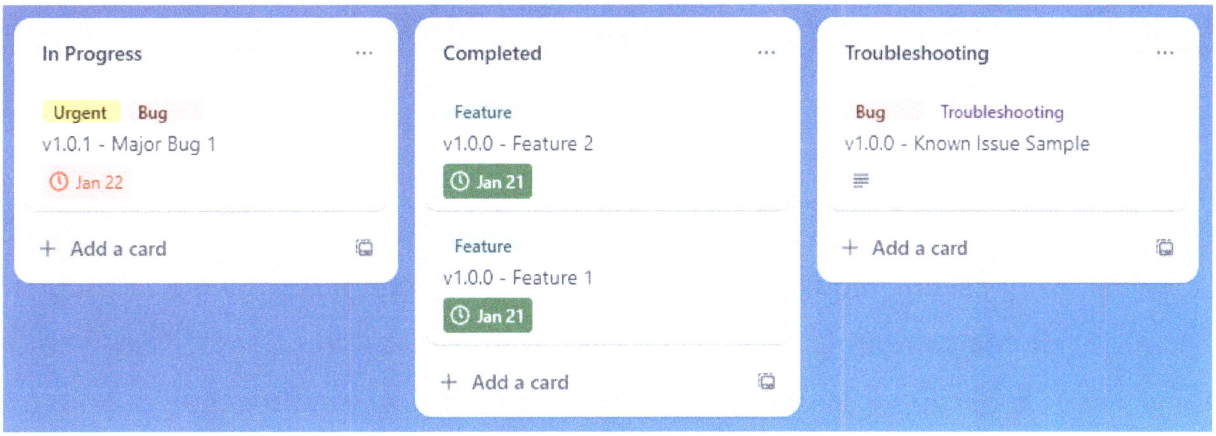

Figure: Troubleshooting Sample

After the "Completed" tasks list, a "Troubleshooting" column was added to document known issues. Any bugs or issues that cannot be fixed at the moment, are documented in this column for future reference. It is important to include the issue description, causes and any workarounds. Later on, this information can be used as a standard reply for related support requests. Here is an example:

v1.0.0 - Known Issue Sample

This issue was identified as a bug on **[third-party software]**, it is caused by **[sample root cause]**. It was already reported to the responsible support team and is currently awaiting for a solution.

Workaround

- Open **[third-party software]** and navigate to **"settings > sample"**
- Change **[property name]** to **[sample value]**
- Save and restart the application

Keep in mind that this workflow is for palliative solutions. As soon as it is possible to eliminate these issues, they should be dealt with, as this will reduce the number of support requests, therefore, reducing the time and effort necessary for product maintenance.

3.4.2. Quality Control

This may seem counterintuitive to beginners, but having a bug free application, doesn't mean it meets the minimum quality standards. Bug free only means your application is not broken, but quality is another beast you must conquer. For example, when people order a dish in a restaurant, it is expected by default, that the food is clean and not contaminated, but the quality of a dish is measured by other factors. For example: Does it taste good? How long does it take to be served? Is the size of the portion reasonable compared to the price? etc. In this context, a bug is like a fly in the soup, it shouldn't be there in the first place, but not being there does not guarantee it is a good soup.

Keep in mind that the attributes that influence the perception of quality vary according to the type of project. For example, from the clients perspective, good quality software should be: useful, reliable, efficient, and easy to use. However, a good quality video game should be: entertaining, visually appealing, performance friendly, fun to play, etc. Quality control consists of measuring and comparing desirable attributes, to ensure the product meets the minimum quality required.

Ideally, quality control should begin in the project planning phase, during the product design stage, and be maintained throughout the development process. However, quality issues are often identified late in development, during the testing phase. While quality issues aren't bugs, major quality issues should be resolved before releasing the first iteration of your product. If, and only if, you are short on time, it is acceptable to add minor quality issues on the roadmap for future versions, but major issues should always be dealt with.

But, keep in mind that the goal of an MVP is not to be perfect, but to be released in an acceptable quality state, so it can be validated by the market. This may seem counterintuitive within the context of quality control, but adopting this mindset will prevent you from getting stuck on an endless polishing cycle, trying to achieve perfection before releasing your product.

3.5. Documentation

Once the polishing phase is complete, the next step is creating the user manual. It should be a simple and straightforward step-by-step guide on how to use the product. Even if you plan on creating video tutorials later on, it is still important to have a user manual as it serves both as a guide and reference material for clients. If you prefer, you may record the tutorials first, and then use screenshots from it to create the user manual, this will make sure they are consistent, but it may push the release date, as recording tutorials usually is more time consuming than creating a text document. Most marketplaces require products to have a PDF user manual included, in order for it to be published, but video tutorials are usually optional, which means that tutorials can be created and published after the product is already live on the store.

If you have created a design document in the planning phase, as recommended, it is good practice to revisit it, to make sure the architecture described on the design document matches the implemented product design. In some situations, adjustments are made on the original design mid development to overcome technical limitations, if any drastic changes are made, the documentation should be updated to match the final design.

Going back to the drawing board at this point may be stressful, as you are most likely already anxious to release the product[31]. However, updating documentation will save you a headache on future updates or, who knows, if ever you hire someone else to work on the project.

[31] Adjustments to the design document can also be made after the product is released to avoid pushing the release date.

Chapter 4: Product Release

If you have made it this far, congratulations, your project is complete! For hobbyists, this may be the top of the mountain. However, for entrepreneurs, it is a small stop to rest and appreciate the view, before continuing on your journey. After all, you still need to release your creation into the world. Either way, be proud of yourself, most people don't get this far.

This chapter focuses on launching digital products on third-party online marketplaces. This is what I do for a living, and I can only teach you how to navigate a path I've already traveled.

4.1. Preparing for Release

As mentioned in the project planning chapter, if you plan to publish on a third-party marketplace, you should be aware of the marketplace's guidelines before creating your product. Once the project is complete and you're ready to publish, it's a good idea to revisit the guidelines as you prepare to submit your product, especially if it's your first product. Some marketplaces review products before approving them for sale. By double-checking the guidelines, you reduce the chances of your product being rejected over minor details.

First step for release is to generate the final build[32] of your product and pack it according to the marketplace file format guidelines. At this point, the product was already tested and polished, but it is recommended to open the final build on the target platform one last time, just to make sure it is working. Files may get corrupted during the build process, so it's better to validate them one final time before uploading them to the target marketplace.

---

[32] "Build" is the term used in the software development industry for the process of compiling and packaging project files into the target format.

Once your project files are ready, it's time to create your product store page. Product pages usually consist of the following information: title, description, category, key images, videos, search tags, pricing, and licensing options.

Having a good product is only half the way. The product page is where potential customers decide whether or not your product is worth investing in. A well-designed product page can be the difference between low and high conversion rates[33]. To be honest, I'm no marketing expert, but here are some best practices I've learned over the years that have helped me increase the conversion rate of my products:

The **product title** should be short, clear, and intuitive. Ideally, just by reading the title, potential customers should be able to identify what the product is about. Including keywords in the title is also a good strategy to increase product discovery and ranking in search results.

For the **product description**, you need to grab attention as soon as possible, start by highlighting what issues and pain points the product solves in the first paragraph, then follow up with a clear description of the product features and benefits. Make it short and straight to the point. Highlighting key selling points using bullet points is also helpful. People have short attention spans, especially regarding textual description, so the idea is to convey the main selling points with the minimum amount of text possible.

Most marketplaces use a **product category** system to facilitate navigation and product discoverability. Select the category that best fits your product. When in doubt between two or more categories, select the one with the highest selling potential. For example, if the product is a vehicle simulation system and there is a category for "systems" and another one for "vehicles", picking the vehicles

[33] Conversion rate is the percentage of store page visitors that bought the product over a period of time. For example, if the product page had 1000 visitors over a month and sold 50 units, that month's conversion rate is 5%.

category may be the better option. The systems category is too broad, which means, people browsing the systems category, may not be interested in vehicles, on the other hand, people browsing the vehicles category are more likely to be interested in a vehicle system.

Key images typically consist of a thumbnail, a banner image, and screenshots. The **thumbnail** is the image that appears in search results alongside other products, so it should be designed to stand out and grab attention. The **banner** is the first image that appears on the product page, so it should be as appealing as possible and clearly display the product name and logo, if any. **Screenshots** should highlight the product's key features and benefits, captions may be included to clearly convey what's being shown in the image. A good trick to save time on the media gallery is to record the product showcase video first, then take screenshots from it.

Some marketplaces support displaying **videos** in the media gallery, alongside screenshots, if not, videos can be posted on third-party platforms and linked to the product description. It is recommended to create at least a **product trailer** and a **features showcase** demo. Given that most people have short attention spans and low tolerance for promotional content, videos should ideally be short and straight to the point. The features showcase must highlight the product's key features and benefits, and may include captions or text banners with relevant information.

Search Tags are keywords related to your product, which are used as search filters and heavily influence search algorithms. Ideally, keywords should be scattered everywhere on the product page, the title, the description, every single text information about the product should include keywords. Nonetheless, most marketplaces also have a dedicated field for adding keywords, try choosing words that are most likely to be searched by people looking for similar products. The selected keywords affect the product's discoverability and search ranking, which strongly impact the product's organic reach.

Each marketplace has its own **licensing options**, which you must be aware of if you intend on hosting your products on a third-party market. However, the **pricing** strategy is up to you. Ideally, the product price should be defined right after finishing the market research, in the project planning phase. As mentioned before, pricing must be taken into consideration in the project feasibility analysis. Imagine wasting months developing a product, just to discover competitors are underpricing the market. Therefore, deciding the price when publishing the product is risky and unwise.

4.2. Product Release

Once the product and the store page are ready, it is time for release. For quality control purposes, most reputable online marketplaces review products before approving them for sale. If that's the case, send your product for review.

By following the marketplace guidelines from the start of the project, as recommended, your product has higher chances of being approved on the first try. But even so, reviewers may still require adjustments before approval. Most of the time, these adjustments are related to small details you overlooked, which can be quickly addressed. However, reviewers may also reject products for unreasonable reasons. For example, questioning product design decisions[34] or any other factors that are not listed in the guidelines. In situations like these, make the pertinent adjustments and resubmit the product for review disputing any claims that don't make sense.

When presenting your case, it is important to be polite and assertive. Remember, the goal is not to prove that you are right, it is to solve any

[34] As a developer, design decisions are up to you. Unless they violate any guidelines, or laws, reviewers have no right to request product redesigns.

misunderstandings and move on. Everyone makes mistakes, including you. Acknowledge your mistakes when you are wrong and make an effort to be professional and polite when pointing out the mistakes of others. Reviewers are human just like you, as long as you remain professional, if you make your case, they may acknowledge the mistake and approve your product.

If your product submission is declined, don't give up on your first try either. Make any necessary adjustments and resubmit it for review. You worked really hard to create your product, as long as it is in accordance with the marketplace guidelines, there are no reasons for it to be rejected. That's why it is really important to study the guidelines before starting the project, and to revisit them before submitting your product for review. By knowing the guidelines better than reviewers themselves, they have no argument to unjustly decline your product.

If, for any reason, your product submission is declined multiple times by different reviewers, that's not a reason to give up either[35]. Consider publishing on other marketplaces or, if you have the funds for it, you may even consider creating your own marketplace. If you've made it this far, you've already conquered the biggest challenge: designing and developing a product.

4.3. Post-Release

Releasing your first product is a major milestone, but if you plan on doing this for a living is not the end of the journey. Nonetheless, this is the birth of your brand and should be taken seriously: you have released your creation into the world and are now responsible for it. But don't worry, being responsible for your creation is not a bad thing, on the contrary, it is something to be proud of.

In the early days after release, you should maximize your marketing efforts and keep an eye for any critical bug reports. If you have the funds, you may

[35] Situations like these are rare, but not impossible.

consider investing in paid ads to generate traction for the product. If it performs well in the early days, it has a greater chance of performing well in the long run, so now is the perfect time to try to get as many people as possible to discover your product. Ideally, you should invest in both paid and organic traffic[36] strategies to redirect leads to your product page.

Purposely increasing organic traffic is a tough challenge, as there are multiple factors involved and they constantly change as technology evolves. For example, organic traffic may be improved by following search engine optimizations best practices (also known as SEO). However, it is not uncommon for updates on search algorithms to flip the rules of the game from time to time.

Therefore, organic traffic optimization requires a continuous effort trying to understand how to leverage the current search algorithms. The main issue with this strategy is that search algorithms are often black boxes, developed and protected by the same companies that profit from selling ads. But don't get me wrong, I'm not saying that you shouldn't try to optimize organic traffic, you definitely should. I'm only telling you the reality that most marketing influencers won't want you to know: the game is not tipped in your favor.

The best organic traffic strategy starts way back on the product design phase: designing a solution for a really annoying problem that affects a large number of people. If you create a solution for an issue like this, you have a higher chance of your product being naturally discovered by this massive market of people desperate to get rid of the problem. Remember, no amount of marketing can turn a bad and useless product into a massive success, on the other hand, a good product may take off on its own, or at least with minimum amount of effort.

---

[36] Organic traffic refers to potential customers, also known as leads, that find your product through non-paid sources.

4.3.1. Video Tutorials

Video tutorials are an extremely powerful tool, as they serve as documentation, generate organic traffic and reduce the amount of effort required for user support, all at the same time. Given that people prefer watching tutorials over reading the user manual, having a tutorial playlist makes your product more attractive for potential customers. The following recommendations and best practices will help you make the most of your tutorials:

- **Tutorial Playlist:** A playlist of short tutorials is more effective than a single long tutorial. Tutorials focused on specific features perform better with SEO[37] strategies and facilitate support requests, as you can link specific tutorials to address customer questions.
- **Video Chapters:** If multiple features are showcased in the same tutorial, separating it into chapters also contributes to SEO and support requests. Chapters make it easier to provide links that start playing at the exact timestamp needed to elucidate questions about specific features.
- **Quick Start Guide:** Ideally, the first tutorial in a playlist should be a quick start guide, showcasing key features and how to use them. This helps users get started on their own and reduces the number of support requests.
- **Voiceover and subtitles:** Voiceover explanations make tutorials clear and easier to understand. Subtitles contribute to SEO and accessibility.
- **Customization Guide:** If the product is customizable, the final tutorial should focus on customization, showcasing features that facilitate the customization process.
- **Optimized Content:** Tutorial content can be optimized to serve both as documentation and marketing material. Here is a recommended structure:

[37] Search Engine Optimization

- **Intro:** Brief description of what is going to be showcased.
- **Call to Action 1:** Where and how to acquire the product.
- **Content:** Step-by-step guide on how to use the features.
- **Call to Action 2:** Invite viewers to engage via the comment section and visit the store page.
- **Outro:** Showcase product and/or company logos.

- **Optimized Description:** A well-written video description may increase both video and product discovery. Here is a recommended structure:
  - **Store Page Link:** Redirect leads directly to the product page.
  - **Description:** Brief description of the product and tutorial contents.
  - **Clickable Chapter List:** Improves navigation and SEO.
  - **Playlist Link:** Access to the entire tutorial playlist.
  - **Contact Information:** Email address, social media links, etc.
- **Cross-linking with Store Page:** Link the tutorial playlist on the product store page description. Having the tutorials and store page pointing to each other, increases the product discoverability and conversion rate.

Chapter 5: Customer Support

As mentioned in chapter one, a catalog of digital products may generate recurring revenue. However, infinite passive income does not exist, even successful products require maintenance in order to thrive and remain relevant over time. Part of the maintenance effort is providing good quality support. Therefore, if you want to be successful, providing quality support is not optional.

This chapter contains guidelines and best practices on how to provide quality support and balance the workload between new projects and support.

5.1. Communication Guidelines

Good communication skills are essential for providing high-quality customer support. Here are some guidelines for good communication:

- Response time should be reasonably fast.
- Be professional and polite (no matter what).
- Grammar matters: mistakes can make you look unprofessional.
- Avoid over-explaining: clear, short and formal answers are the way to go.
- Express gratitude for feedback, suggestions and bug reports[38].
- No false promises: be honest about your product's current features and the features you intend to add in the future.
- Be friendly and helpful, but set clear boundaries about what is and what is not included in your services.

[38] Receiving a bug report may be disappointing, but this also means the customer took the time to inform you, giving you the opportunity to improve your product, so be thankful for that.

- In conflict situations, deescalating is always the best option. However, if that is not possible, contact an impartial third party for mediation[39].
- Use automated replies to inform customers about expected response times and communication guidelines.
- If, for some reason, support is suspended for a period of time, set an automated reply to inform why and when it's going to come back. Most people don't mind waiting, as long as you don't keep them in the dark.
- Your email signature is the equivalent of a digital business card, optimize it by adding marketplace links alongside the contact information.
- Having a Q&A section on the product store page, tends to reduce the number of pre-purchase questions.
- Video tutorials tend to reduce the number of support requests.
- Message templates can be used to decrease response time.

5.2. Communication Channels

Sellers are required to provide at least a support email address when creating a profile on any online marketplace. Other communication channels are usually optional, but may also be included to increase your communication network. After your first product goes live, all communications channels should be monitored on a daily basis, on business days, to check for new messages. Most messages fall into one of the following three categories: Pre-purchase Questions, Support Requests or Spam.

---

[39] For example, if a rude customer is making unreasonable demands or leaves an unfair negative review, you may appeal to the marketplace support team. If you've remained reasonable and polite throughout the conversation, chances are in your favor.

5.2.1. Pre-Purchase Questions

Pre-purchase questions come from potential customers interested in your products. These usually don't require much time and effort to be replied, all you need to do is to be honest about the product current features and limitations, and what is included in the roadmap for future versions. Ideally, these should be answered as fast as possible, to increase your chances of closing the sale.

5.2.2. Support Requests

The amount of support request generated by a product is directly proportional to its usability and stability. Unstable products tend to receive many bug reports, while poor usability, generates confusion and increases the number of customer questions. In order to minimize support requests, the product should be designed to be as intuitive and as easy to use as possible, it must also be thoroughly tested to ensure a stable release. Nonetheless, eliminating all support requests is virtually impossible. There will always be an issue or someone with a question. Since every support request has the potential to become either a positive or a negative review, they must be analyzed and handled properly.

For solo developers, I highly recommend strategically centralizing support requests in a single communication channel, preferably an email address.

Advantages of email support requests

- Automatically saves a history of all support requests that can be easily filtered by sender.
- Email messages are not expected to be replied right away, which gives you time to analyze the issue and prepare a proper response.
- Trustworthy email providers perform security scans on attachments automatically and display warnings about suspicious links or files.

- Email supports images intercalated with text, which is extremely useful for step-by-step guides or detailed explanations.
- If needed, the entire email thread can be exported into a single PDF file.

For paid products, it is heavily recommended to request proof of purchase before proceeding with support requests, especially when dealing with digital products. Providing good quality support requires a lot of time and effort. Solo developers have limited resources that need to be allocated between new projects and providing support for real customers. Therefore, solo developers cannot afford wasting time providing support for illegal downloads. Although this may seem a bit harsh, if you're not careful with your time you may get stuck serving people that do not respect you as a professional.

Support requests about usability related questions can be handled by sending a brief explanation or step-by-step guide on how to use the product. If the topic is already covered in a video tutorial, you may also recommend watching the respective tutorial for further information. If the topic is covered in the user manual, you may copy and paste the answer to save time, as it is common for customers to open a support request before referring to the user manual. If the topic is not covered in the user manual nor tutorials, and you notice it is a recurring question, you may create a troubleshooting[40] to document the answer, in order to reduce the time spent replying to the same question in the future. Recurring usability questions, may also be a sign that some features are not intuitive enough, which may be addressed on future updates.

For bug reports, the first step is to validate if the reported issue is really a bug. Sometimes, customers that are not familiarized with the product, may misunderstand functionalities and report them as bugs. Situations like these can be solved with a brief explanation and elucidation of any follow-up question.

[40] Recurring pre-purchase questions may be documented on the Q&A section in the product store page. However, recurring usability questions should be documented internally as troubleshootings.

However, if the issue is indeed confirmed to be a bug, the first thing you should do is to apologize for the inconvenience and thank the customer for reporting the issue. This is not only the most professional course of action, but also a very effective strategy for appeasing the customer while you take action to solve the issue. Any major or critical issues should be prioritized and fixed as soon as possible through patches or hotfixes. As for minor issues, fixing them right away will improve the product stability and leave a good impression on the reporting customer, which may lead to a positive review.

However, if your schedule is tight, minor issues may be added on the roadmap to be solved on a future update. Regardless if it is a major or minor issue, once it is fixed, get back to the customer to let them know it was solved. This post-fix follow-up contact is a good opportunity for asking for a review. Customers are more likely to leave a positive review after receiving support[41], especially if you have taken action to fix the reported issue.

5.2.3. Spam & Other Shady Messages

After publishing your first product, you will start receiving a lot of spam and other shady messages. For security reasons, the best you can do is ignore, report as spam and delete these messages. Do not open, do not reply, do not access any links nor open any files. Most cyber attacks require the victim to interact with the attacker in order to be successful, not interacting at all is the safest thing you can do. Keep your distance from scammers and enable every security feature available to safeguard your business accounts.

5.2.4. Communication Strategy

Working on a new project while simultaneously managing communication for all previously published products can be challenging for solo developers.

[41] This is not exclusive for bug reports, it applies to all support requests.

Communication is essential for product catalog maintenance, which then translates into cash flow. On the other hand, new products and updates are essential for business growth. Therefore, in a healthy business, communication and development must walk side by side.

Luckily, the amount of messages generated by a product is directly proportional to its success. By the time the messages generated by a product becomes impossible to reply by a single person, most likely, the product is already generating enough revenue to hire a support team[42]. Provided, of course, that you have properly monetized your product. However, before reaching this stage, solo developers need to handle development and communication by themselves. Therefore, communication needs to be as efficient as possible. The less time you spend on communication, more time may be allocated on new projects.

The following communication strategy has 3 clear goals and 4 simple steps:

Communication Goals

- Reply all messages within a reasonable response time.
- Convert the maximum number of pre-purchase questions into sales.
- Improve customer satisfaction by providing high-quality support.

Communication Strategy

- **Step 1 - Daily Task Management:** Once you have a product in the market, communication becomes a daily task in your routine. The top priority at the start of your working day is not opening your current project, it is checking for new messages.

[42] If you eventually reach this point, you may also consider pausing the development of new products, to focus your attention on the successful ones.

- **Step 2 - Prioritization by Message Type:** Before replying, read all incoming messages and separate pre-purchase questions from support requests. Since pre-purchase questions are faster to reply than support requests, replying them first eliminates the most amount of messages in a shorter period of time. Then, reply to all support requests that are missing key information, politely requesting for it to be provided. Lastly, analyze and reply to all support requests that have all the information needed to proceed, these are the most time consuming, therefore leaving them for last is the most efficient strategy. Summarizing:
    - Read all messages before replying.
    - Separate pre-purchase questions from support requests.
    - Reply all pre-purchase questions
    - Request missing information on incomplete support requests.
        - Proof of purchase for paid products.
        - Screenshots, videos, software version, etc.
    - Analyze and reply to all remaining support requests.
- **Step 3 - Marketing:** Marketing is an integral part of the communication strategy. No one is going to message you about your product, if they don't even know it exists. Paid traffic strategies can be easily automated, however, organic traffic requires continuous effort. It may be a single social media post, publishing a short video of a product, or a devlog of your next project. If you remain consistent, small daily efforts make a difference in the long run.
- **Step 4 - Resume Development:** Once the daily communication tasks are completed, allocate the rest of your working hours into new projects.

The main benefit of this strategy is that it automatically balances the allocation of time between communication and the development of new projects, based on how much attention your products are getting in the market. If you start receiving many messages, most likely one of your products is about to become a success, so you need to focus your attention on it to maximize the results. None or few messages, it's an indication that you need to create more products, since you spend less time on communication, you have more time for development.

5.3. Message Template Samples

Message templates can be strategically used to reduce the time spent replying pre-purchase questions and support requests. Here are some templates samples, based on what I use in my daily routine. Note that placeholder text was used for sample purposes.

5.3.1. Social Media Automated Response

[Automatic Reply]

Thanks for getting in touch. Response time is usually within 24 hours on business days.

[IMPORTANT]

Support requests are now being handled exclusively by email. If you need support, please send a message to **support@sample.com**

You support request must contain the following information:

- Marketplace Invoice Number
- Detailed description of the issue
- Screenshots of the issue (if possible)

5.3.2. Pre-Purchase Questions

Thank you for your interest in **[product_name]**.

Yes, it does support **[sample feature]**. Here is a tutorial on how it works: **[tutorial link].**

[sample feature] is not supported, due to **[brief explanation].**

[sample feature] is not supported yet, but there are plans to include this feature in a future version. Thank you for your suggestion.

If you have more questions, please let me know.

5.3.3. Support Request Proof of Purchase

I apologise for the inconvenience, but in order to proceed with your support request, I'll need you to provide the following information:

- Marketplace Invoice Number
- **[other missing pertinent information]**

5.3.4. Bug Report

Thank you for reporting this issue.

I'll take a closer look and get back to you with more information as soon as possible.

Meanwhile, if you have any questions, please let me know.

5.3.5. Bug Patch

> Thank you for your patience regarding this matter,
>
> The issue was identified and fixed. I'm sending you a patch.
> Here is a step-by-step guide on how to apply it: **[...]**
>
> Please follow up to confirm the patch was successfully applied.

5.3.6. Bug Resolution

> Thank you for confirming the issue was fixed.
>
> An official update patch is expected to go live in **[expected release]**.
>
> Once again, thank you for reporting the issue.
>
> If you haven't already, please leave a review to support my work.

5.3.7. Third Party Bug Report

> Thank you for reporting this issue.
>
> It was identified as a bug on **[third party platform name]** and has been reported to the responsible support team.
>
> In the meantime, here is a possible workaround: **[step-by-step explanation]**
>
> If you have any questions, please let me know.
>
> If you haven't already, please leave a review to support my work.

5.3.8. Usability Questions

> Thank you for acquiring **[product name]**.
>
> Regarding your questions,
>
> **[brief explanation]**
>
> Here is a tutorial with a step-by-step guide: **[tutorial link]**
>
> For more information, please refer to section **[section number]** of the user manual.
>
> If you haven't already, please leave a review to support my work.

5.3.9. Email Signature Sample

> **Follow me to get notified about new releases**
>
> Unity Asset Store | FAB Unreal Marketplace | Discord | Instagram | Twitter | Youtube
>
> **Warley - WSM Game Studio**
> wsmgamestudio@gmail.com
> wsmgamestudio.com

5.4. Dealing with Piracy

Any product that gets the attention of the market, has a really high chance of eventually being leaked on piracy websites. It doesn't matter if it is from a big company or a small indie dev trying to make a living, people just don't care.

Some people refuse to pay for digital products no matter what, and unfortunately, there are also people trying to profit from the hard work of others. In the end, the reason piracy exists is not that complicated: when supply meets demand, a new market is born, even if it is a shady one.

If it comes to your attention that your product has been leaked, don't even access the website and, most importantly, never download the files to confirm that it is really your product. Allegedly, some piracy websites use leaked products as bait and profit either by displaying shady ads all over the page or by injecting malware into the files. Unless you have a solid background on cybersecurity, downloading the files even for validation purposes may put you at risk.

Piracy is a reality of the digital industry, big companies have been fighting it for years with little to no success. Taking down a piracy website or trying to force the removal of a product requires a lot of time, effort, money and bureaucracy. And even when it works, nothing prevents the product from being leaked again, by the same person, somewhere else. As a solo developer, the best you can do is just ignore it. There will always be people that prefer acquiring products on the official website. Those are your real customers, your time is better spent providing good support and creating good products for them[43].

---

[43] Don't be afraid to politely request proof of purchase before providing support. Real customers won't be offended by this.

Chapter 6: Final Considerations

Since you've made it to the end of the book, as a reward, here is a bonus tip: Use upsell strategies on your product catalog. This can be done by designing multiple products that are compatible with each other and selling them both individually and as part of product bundles[44]. This not only increases your sales, but also makes your catalog more consistent and professional.

Thank you for reading this book. If you are reading this right now, it means I have made it to the end of my first book project. Every project is a journey, if you prepare yourself and remain faithful to your goals, you may eventually reach the top of the mountain. I'm still climbing my own mountain, this book is just another step towards the top. If by sharing my humble experiences, your journey becomes at least a bit safer and easier than mine, for me this book is already a success. If our paths cross during our journeys, feel free to stop by to say hello. You can check my progress and find my contact information on my company website: https://wsmgamestudio.com/.

If you haven't started your journey yet, well, what are you waiting for? Today is the first day of the rest of your life. It doesn't matter what happened in your past, the decisions you make today are the only thing capable of creating a brighter future.

[44] There are other upsell strategies, this is just one example that applies to the product catalog business strategy.

www.ingramcontent.com/pod-product-compliance
Lightning Source LLC
Chambersburg PA
CBHW061224240926
51846CB00006B/1344
9786501645605